SOCIAL POLICY:

AN ANARCHIST RESPONSE

By the same author

Anarchy in Action
Streetwork: The Exploding School (with Anthony Fyson)
Vandalism
Tenants Take Over
Housing: An Anarchist Approach
The Child in the City
Art and the Built Environment (with Eileen Adams) .
Arcadia for All (with Dennis Hardy)
When We Build Again
Goodnight Campers (with Dennis Hardy)
Chartres: The Making of a Miracle
The Allotment: Its Landscape and Culture (with David Crouch)
The Child in the Country
Undermining the Central Line (with Ruth Rendell)
Welcome, Thinner City: Urban Survival in the 1990s
Images of Childhood (with Tim Ward)
Talking Houses
Talking Schools
Freedom to Go: After the Motor Age
Influences: Voices of Creative Dissent
New Town, Home Town
Talking to Architects
Reflected in Water: a crisis of social responsibility
Havens and Springboards
Sociable Cities (with Peter Hall)

FREEDOM PRESS publish *Freedom* (fortnightly) and *The Raven* (quarterly) as well as books (more than sixty titles in print).

FREEDOM PRESS BOOKSHOP carries the most comprehensive stock of anarchist literature including titles from North America. Please send for our current list.

Freedom Press, in Angel Alley, 84b Whitechapel High Street,
London E1 7QX

SOCIAL POLICY
an anarchist response

by Colin Ward

FREEDOM PRESS
LONDON

First published in 1996 by the London School of Economics

Published in Italian in 1998 as
La Città dei Ricchi e la Città dei Poveri
by Edizioni e/o

This edition, with corrections, published by
FREEDOM PRESS
84b Whitechapel High Street
London E1 7QX
2000

ISBN 0 900384 98 0

Typeset by Jayne Clementson
Printed in Great Britain by Aldgate Press, London E1 7RQ

Contents

Introduction

Colin Ward, Britain's leading anarchist philosopher, was visiting Centenary Professor in the Department of Social Policy at the London School of Economics during 1995/6.

Colin Ward built his reputation in the 1960s as editor of *Anarchy*, hailed by Colin MacInnes as "the liveliest social commentary in Britain". He has published many books, articles and pamphlets since the 1970s, among the best known of which are *Child in the City*, *Anarchy in Action*, *Tenants Take Over*, *Goodnight Campers* and *The Allotment*.

His primary concerns are housing and the environment, but these fit within his broad commitment to anarchist ideas.

His lectures on the history of informal housing movements at the London School of Economics were very popular with students. This volume includes those lectures and we are delighted to publish the texts of all his talks during his year with us.

Special thanks to Becky Tunstall, Michael Bentham and Professor David Downes who made the lectures and this volume possible.

Anne Power
October 1996

The welfare road we failed to take

Every writer produces, every now and then, a phrase, a sentence or a paragraph, which to his or her immense gratification, other people quote. I have been writing for all my adult life, for propagandist reasons, so I frequently recycle other people's words, quite apart from my own, and I too, have a most-quoted paragraph, which I first used, I think, in a letter to *The Listener* in 1960 and recycled in 1973 in my book *Anarchy in Action*, which I am happy to say is endlessly translated and reprinted.

It expresses a commonplace of social history with which a specialist audience like you will be thoroughly familiar, but which perhaps is or was less well-known in the outside world. My most-quoted paragraph was this:

> "When we compare the Victorian antecedents of our public institutions with the organs of working-class mutual aid in the same period, the very names speak volumes. On the one side the Workhouse, the Poor Law Infirmary, the National Society for the Education of the Poor in Accordance with the Principles of the Established Church; and on the other, the *Friendly* Society, the Sick *Club*, the *Co-operative* Society, the Trade *Union*. One represents the tradition of fraternal and autonomous associations springing up from below, the other that of authoritarian institutions directed from above."

Now my quotable paragraph stresses a truth that has been ignored by socialists for generations, but it also relates to a question that students of politics have been asking themselves since 1979, which is that of the failure of British socialism to win the hearts of the British public.

In this connection, the paragraph that *I* frequently quote comes from Fabian Tract No. 4 called *What Socialism Is*, published in 1886. The anonymous introduction to that text remarked that:

"English Socialism is not yet Anarchist or Collectivist,
nor yet defined enough in point of policy to be classified.
There is a mass of Socialistic feeling not yet conscious of
itself as Socialism. But when the unconscious Socialists
of England discover their position, they also will probably
fall into two parties; a Collectivist party supporting a
strong central administration and a counterbalancing
Anarchist party defending individual initiative against
that administration."

I have always found that to be an extraordinarily interesting unfulfilled
prophecy, not because anyone would have expected an anarchist
'party' in the ordinary sense to have emerged, but because it was
evident over a century ago that there were other paths to socialism
beside the electoral struggle for power over the centralised state. It is
also interesting because of its assumption that anarchism was
individualistic as opposed to the collectivism of Fabian socialists.

Now the one celebrated anarchist thinker with whom the early
Fabians were personally acquainted was Peter Kropotkin. In fact, in
that same year, 1886, he and a Fabian, Charlotte Wilson, were to
start the anarchist journal *Freedom*, which of course exists to this
day, and was then subtitled 'A Journal of Anarchist-Communism'.
His ideology was the very opposite of individualism, and his most
famous book, *Mutual Aid: A Factor of Evolution*, was a long and
detailed celebration of co-operation as the condition for survival in
any species, in opposition to the so-called 'social Darwinists' and the
dogma of the war of each against all.

In a later book, *Modern Science and Anarchism*, he declared that
"the economic and political liberation of man will have to create new
forms for its expression in life, instead of those established by the
State". For he thought it self-evident that "this new form will have
to be more popular, more decentralised, and nearer to the folk-mote
self-government than representative government can ever be",
reiterating that we will be compelled to find new forms of organisation
for the social functions that the state fulfils through the bureaucracy,
and that "as long as this is not done, nothing will be done".

Part of Kropotkin's argument, and mine, is that in the nineteenth
century the newly-created British working class built up from
nothing a vast network of social and economic initiatives based on

self-help and mutual aid. The list is endless: friendly societies, building societies, sick clubs, coffin clubs, clothing clubs, up to enormous federated enterprises like the trade union movement and the Co-operative movement. The question that latter-day re-discoverers of that tradition ask is, 'How did we allow it to ossify?'

The Indian politician Jayaprakash Narayan used to say that Gandhi used up all the moral oxygen in India, so the British Raj suffocated. In exactly the same way, I would claim that the political left in this country invested all its fund of social inventiveness in the idea of the state, so that its own traditions of self-help and mutual aid were stifled for lack of ideological oxygen. How on earth did British socialists allow these concepts to be hijacked by the political right, since it is these human attributes, and not the state and its bureaucracies, that actually hold human society together?

Politically, it was because of the implicit alliance of Fabians and Marxists, both of whom believed completely in the state, and assumed that they would be the particular elite in control of it. Administratively it was because of the alliance of bureaucrats and professionals: the British civil service and the British professional classes, with their undisguised contempt for the way ordinary people organised anything. I have been reading Ralf Dahrendorf's history of the LSE and have reached his account of the Minority Report of the Royal Commission on the Poor Law from 1909. He remarks that:

> "what followed from the Minority Report was a welfare state with specialised public agencies for every need: health and housing, education and unemployment, disability and old age. There were many reasons to be sceptical. Some undoubtedly preferred the status quo to the 'socialism' of a welfare state of this kind; others abhorred the bureaucratic nightmare and the rule of unaccountable 'experts'."

However, that document set the pattern realised after 1945. The great tradition of working-class self-help and mutual aid was written off, not just as irrelevant, but as an actual impediment, by the political and professional architects of the welfare state, aspiring to a universal public provision of everything for everybody. The contribution that the recipients had to make to all this theoretical bounty was ignored as a mere embarrassment – apart, of course, from paying for it. The nineteenth century working classes, living far below the tax threshold, taxed themselves in pennies every week for the upkeep of their innumerable friendly societies. The twentieth century employed workers, as well as its alleged National Insurance contributions, pays a large slice of its income for the support of the state. The socialist ideal was rewritten as a world in which everyone was entitled to everything, but where nobody except the providers had any actual say about anything. We have been learning for years, in the anti-welfare backlash, what a very vulnerable utopia that was.

History itself was re-interpreted to suit the managerial, political and bureaucratic vision. The medical historian Roy Porter remarks that "Beatrice Webb admitted doctoring the presentation of her evidence on friendly societies for the 1909 report", as though everybody knew this. And what is taught about the origins of the welfare state implies that twentieth century state universalism replaced the pathetic unofficial or voluntary and patchy pioneering ventures of the nineteenth century. However, in the past 25 years or so, a new interest in popular history, exemplified by the History Workshop movement and the boom in local and oral history, has uncovered buried layers of our past.

Take education as an example. We have absorbed the official line that it was only rivalry between religious bodies that delayed until 1870 (and in effect 1880 or later) universal, free and compulsory elementary education. A centenary publication from the National Union of Teachers (*The Struggle for Education*, 1970) said that "apart from religious and charitable schools, 'dame' or common schools were operated by the private enterprise of people who were often barely literate", and it explained the widespread working class hostility to the school boards with the remark that "parents were not always quick to appreciate the advantages of full-time schooling against the loss of extra wages". But recent historians have shown the resistance to state schooling in a quite different light. Stephen Humphries is the author of *Hooligans or Rebels? An Oral History of Working Class Childhood and Youth 1889-1939* (first published by Basil Blackwell in 1981 and just reprinted). He finds that these private schools, by the 1860s, "were providing an alternative education for approximately one-third of all working-class children" and suggests that:

"This enormous demand for private as opposed to public education is perhaps best illustrated by the fact that working-class parents in a number of major cities responded to the introduction of compulsory attendance regulation not by sending their children to provided state schools, as government had predicted, but by extending the length of their child's education in private schools. Parents favoured these schools for a number of reasons: They were small and close to home and were consequently more personal and more convenient that most publicly provided schools; they were informal, tolerant of irregular attendance and unpunctuality; no attendance registers were kept; they were not segregated according to age and sex; they used individual as opposed to authoritarian teaching methods; and, most important, they belonged to, and were controlled by, the local community rather than being imposed on the neighbourhood by an alien authority."

This dissenting interpretation of the history of schooling was reinforced with a mass of statistical evidence in a subsequent book by Philip Gardner, *The Lost Elementary Schools of Victorian England* (Croom Helm, 1984). He found that what he called working-class schools, set up by working-class people in working-class neighbourhoods, "achieved just what the customers wanted: quick results in basic skills like reading, writing and arithmetic, wasted no time on religious studies and moral uplift, and represented a genuinely alternative approach to childhood learning to that prescribed by the education experts". When the historian Paul Thompson discussed the implications of this book in *New Society* (6th December 1984) he concluded that the price of eliminating those schools had been "the suppression in countless working-class children of the very appetite for education and ability to learn independently which contemporary progressive education seeks to rekindle". Since he wrote, of course, the Department of Education has sought to extinguish the concept of progressive education.

Another field where the excavation of previously distorted history has yielded surprising facts is that of medicine. Now I am old enough to have been an employed worker under the pre-NHS system of panel doctors and 'approved societies', so of course I know that it was a comprehensive and free-at-the-point-of delivery system provided that you were an employed worker, with no prescription charge and no charge for dentistry for example.

I also know that it wasn't the Thatcher government which set about reorganising the NHS. It has been in a state of continuous reorganisation since its inception. Like you, I have heard former employees of the expensive consultants McKinsey's, confessing that the advice they gave was bad advice, just as I have heard Mr William Tatton-Brown, the former chief architect to the Department of Health, confessing that the advice he had given on the distribution, size and design of hospitals was also wrong.

In this area I can't improve on Ivan Illich's conclusions about the professionalisation of knowledge:

> "It makes people dependent on having their knowledge produced for them. It leads to a paralysis of the moral and political imagination ... Over-confidence in 'better knowledge' becomes a self-fulfilling prophecy. People first cease to trust their own judgement and then want to be told the truth about what they know. Over-confidence in 'better decision-making' first hampers people's ability to decide for themselves and then undermines their belief that they can decide."

Consequently, ten years ago I was happy to read the book by David Green, who had recently been a Labour councillor in Newcastle-upon-Tyne, called *Working-Class Patients and the Medical Establishment: Self-Help in Britain from the Mid-Nineteenth Century to 1948* (Gower/Temple 1986). His study of self-governing working-class medical societies showed that the self-organisation of patients provided a rather better degree of consumer control of medical services than had been achieved in post-Lloyd George and post-Bevan days. Not the least of the virtues of that book was that, as Roy Porter noted, "he takes that hallowed belief of progressives – that the improvement of the people's health hinges on state intervention – challenges its historical accuracy, and questions whether it is, in any case, a good doctrine for the Left to hold" (*New Society*, 28th February 1986).

I first met David Green only recently, at a seminar organised by Demos, and learned that there was no place for him on the political Left, since he was talking as Director of the Health and Welfare Unit at the Institute of Economic Affairs. I must add that his recent book *Reinventing Civil Society* (IEA, 1993) is a criticism, not a defence of Thatcherism. But it is also a criticism of the automatic assumptions of the political Left and its faith in the State.

Since most of us gather more information from television than from books, it is worth noting that more people were set thinking about the issues involved by Peter Hennessey's Channel 4 series called *What Has Become of Us*. In preparation for his book *Never Again* he talked to retired miners in the shadow of a statue of Aneurin Bevan. They had been members of the Tredegar Medical Aid Society, founded in 1870, which provided medical and hospital care for everyone in the district, whether or not they were among the nine million people who were members of mutual aid societies among the twelve million covered by the 1911 Act. They told Hennessey that "We thought he was turning the whole country into one big Tredegar".

On the day I met David Green, *The Independent* (3rd April 1995) chanced to have a story about the final demise of this body. This explained that it "sustained itself through the years by voluntary contributions of three old pennies in the pound from the wage-packets of miners and steelworkers ... At one time the society employed five doctors, a dentist, a chiropodist and a physiotherapist" and of course a hospital "to care for the health of about 25,000 people".

Why didn't the whole country become, not one big Tredegar, but a network of Tredegars? The answer is that all parties became advocates of what that anonymous Fabian pamphleteer of 110 years ago called "a strong central administration", or what the philosopher Martin Buber called "the political surplus" of the state over society. There is no room for self-taxation in a state where the treasury of central government has a virtual monopoly of revenue-gathering. When every employed worker in Tredegar paid a voluntary levy of three old pence in the pound, the earnings of even high-skilled industrial workers were below the liability to income tax. But ever since PAYE was introduced in the second world war, the Treasury has creamed off the cash which once supported local initiatives. If the pattern of local self-taxation on the Tredegar model really had become the universal pattern for health provision, it would not have become the plaything of central government financial policy.

As it is, of course, the affluent can buy private health care, though neither BUPA nor the NHS can be described as user-controlled. There once was the option of universal health provision 'at the point of service' if only Fabians, Marxists and Aneurin Bevan had trusted the state and centralised revenue-gathering and policy-making less, and our capacity for self-help and mutual aid more.

I deliberately refrain from advancing parallel arguments about housing, since I have produced endless articles and half a dozen books on this theme in the past quarter of a century.

Now the standard argument against a localist and decentralist point of view, is that of universalism: an equal service to all citizens, which it is thought that central control achieves. The short answer to this is that it doesn't!

We have all learned how in the early 1920s George Lansbury and Poplar Borough councillors went to jail for refusing to pay the poor rate demanded from them, when far richer boroughs paid less. Isn't it still true today that the Council Tax is higher in London's poorest boroughs than in its richest ones? When I was a child certain parts of the country were designated as Depressed Areas, for extra central government aid. Later the names were changed to Special Areas or Assisted Areas. Despite decades of special redistributive policy they are still the poorest parts of the country. Standards of provision *do* vary despite years of allegiance to universalist policies. I live deep in the country in an affluent area, midway between two large towns. Doctors refer patients to the big hospitals in Town A or Town B, but you can hear from patients that they have very different reputations, which often relate to individual departments. The same user opinion obviously applies to schools too.

I think it is time to admit that universalism is an unattainable idea in a society that is enormously divided in terms of income and access to employment. We would do better to look at a society which turns British assumptions upside down. I am talking about Switzerland, which considers itself to be a welfare society rather than a welfare state. I do not suggest that the Swiss Confederation is anything like an anarchist society. (Thanks to the fact that it has a Freedom of Information Act, my anarchist friends there have applied for their secret police records, which even with many blacked-out pages, are impressively long.)

But in that country, where voluntary bodies for every conceivable purpose proliferate, the revenue-gathering body is the *commune*, large or small, grudgingly passes over some cash to the *cantons*, which passes on some to the *federal council*. What I learn from students of the Swiss system like Ioan Bowen Rees in *Government by Community* (Chas. Knight & Co., 1971) or Jonathan Steinberg in *Why Switzerland?* (Cambridge, 1976, 1996), is that the civic sense there is so well-developed a tradition that the rich communes come to the rescue of the poor communes, out of a sense of social responsibility.

I attribute the fact that this is inconceivable in Britain to the fact that we stifled the localist and voluntarist approach in favour of conquest of the power of the state. We took the wrong road to welfare.

The appalling problem, for you as much as for me, is the question of how we get back on the mutual aid road *instead of* commercial health insurance and private pension schemes. We have all watched the eagerness with which Building Societies have turned themselves into banks and shed the last vestiges of their origins as mutual friendly societies. Similarly we have seen the retail co-operative movement shaking off its history faced by the inroads into its market by its capitalist rivals.

As the official welfare edifice, patiently built up by the Fabians and Beveridge, becomes merely the safety-net for the poor who can't afford anything better, the likeliest slow renewal of the self-help and mutual aid principle seems to me to emerge form the new so-called underclass of those people rejected by the economy in alliance with those déclassé people who just can't stomach current economic and social values. I am thinking of marginal activities like food co-ops, credit unions, tenant self-management, and LETS (Local Exchange Trading Systems).

Huge welfare networks were built up by the poor in the rise of industrial Britain. Perhaps they will be rebuilt, out of the same sheer necessity during its decline. What do you think?

References and Sources

(1886) *What Socialism Is*, Fabian Tract No. 4, Fabian Society: London.

Peter Kropotkin (1987), *Mutual Aid: A Factor of Evolution*, Freedom Press, (Heinemann: London, 1992).

Stephen Humphries (1981,1996) *Hooligans or Rebels? An Oral History of Working Class Childhood and Youth 1889-1939*, Basil Blackwell: Oxford.

Philip Gardner (1984), *The Lost Elementary Schools of Victorian England* Croom Helm: London.

Paul Thompson (1984) *New Society*, 6 Dec.

Roy Porter in (1986) *New Society*, 28 Feb.

David Green (1985) *Working-Class Patients and the Medical Establishment: Self-Help in Britain from the Mid-Nineteenth Century to 1948*, Gower/Temple: Aldershot.

David Green (1993) *Reinventing Civil Society*, Institute of Economic Affairs, Health and Welfare Unit: London.

Ioan Bowen Rees (1971) *Government by Community* Chas. Knight: London.

Jonathan Steinberg (1976, 1996) *Why Switzerland?*, Cambridge University Press: Cambridge.

Colin Ward (1973) *Anarchy In Action*, Allen & Unwin: London (Freedom Press, 1982, 1996).

The hidden social history of housing

1. Cotters and squatters: informal settlements of the eighteenth and nineteenth centuries

My purpose in these four seminars is to explore aspects of the history of housing, in terms of housing based on local and popular initiative, self-help and mutual aid. It is important to remember that most of the world's population lives in houses built by themselves, their parents and grandparents and that the world's most widely-used building materials are grass in its various forms from straw to bamboo, and mud in its innumerable forms from rammed earth to brick.

But the history of housing is a history of legislation, or of the landlord and tenant's relationship, or of housing standards. I learned from the architect John Turner three universal laws of housing, the second of which was that the important thing about housing is not what it *is*, but what it *does* in people's lives, in other words that dweller satisfaction is not necessarily related to the imposition of standards.

There always was an alternative history of housing, exemplified for most people by Gerrard Winstanley's 'ideologically-inspired squat' at St George's Hill at Walton-on-Thames in Surrey in 1649. He, like many others, believed that there had been common access to land until the Norman Conquest in 1066. The corollary belief was that every last acre of the country had a legal landlord, which was true in theory, but was modified by the concept of common rights and by the fact that there are limitations to every system of bureaucracy. There were always places where people did their own thing.

In English history, the key historical fact that we have to grapple with was that of the Enclosure of the common fields, common lands and wastes, which was not a sudden transformation in the eighteenth

century, but a continuous process over centuries, culminating in the
Parliamentary enclosures of, say, 1750 to 1850. They had different
effects on the rural poor, who were of course, the vast majority of the
population, in different places, and my generation learned about
them in the primary school in the early 1930s from the progressive
history textbooks of the day, the Piers Plowman Histories which
derived their material on this topic from the most famous account,
The Village Labourer by J.L. and Barbara Hammond, first published
in 1911. They in turn relied on the pioneering researches of Slater,
Unwin and Hasbach from an earlier decade, on the fate of the
English peasantry.

I absorbed as a child the view that the loss of rights by the poor was
devastating, but then a new generation of historians urged us to
believe that the change was 'historically necessary' to produce the
new urban working class through migration and to increase the
productivity of agriculture, by the archaic system of the common
fields and by poor people's rights over the 'wastes' which in the days
when, as Griffiths Cunningham put it "vast stretches of the English
countryside were 'no-man's land' in the real sense of the word,
provided a livelihood for the rural poor".

A later school of historians contradicted the Hammond
interpretation, using words which K.D.M. Snell in his *Annals of the
Labouring Poor*, gathered from the writings of G.E. Mingay, like
'mistaken', 'exaggerated', 'overdrawn', 'unrealistic', 'unhistorical',
'partial and tendentious', 'seriously astray', 'biased', and 'illiberal',
only to be followed by a further group of scholars, the counter-
revisionists, who have re-certified the older point of view. One of
them, the same Dr Snell, considers that the most recent reappraisal
of open-field agriculture has established "that the open fields were
far more open to innovative and flexible agriculture than once
supposed", and that "the account of them as seriously backward and
by nature inhibitive of new techniques is most certainly incorrect".

But there were plenty of places, particularly in the hinterland of
towns where the process of enclosure was less important than the
accessibility of small patches of land where a living could be made in
a variety of industries meeting the needs of town-dwellers, whether
in keeping chickens or cows, growing vegetables, or in quarrying
stone or making bricks, or taking in laundry for town dwellers.

In reading the landscape whether on the ground or on the map, there is an old and useful classification of parishes, that of 'open' and 'close' villages. We associate the 'close' village with a single land-owner who, through his agents, and his links with other institutions like law-enforcement and the Church, controls everything that happens. This is the village celebrated in the currently-favoured Heritage interpretation of history, based on the Great House, visited in droves and publicised by the National Trust, and the idea of paternal stewardship of the land and its occupiers. The 'open' village is straggling, unpredictable parish with plenty of evidence of owner-built housing, of mixed occupations, and non-conformity, all of them associated with the dispersal of land ownership. There is a very nice passage in *The Penguin Guide to the Landscape of England and Wales* by Paul Coones and John Patten (yes, the Conservative politician, now dismissed, who started life as a geography teacher). They remark that:

> "In order to sense the atmosphere of the pre-industrial rural scene it is desirable to leave the beaten track (as far as this is still possible) and seek out those corners of England and Wales where odd vestiges of that vanished era can be glimpsed. Such places are usually quiet and sheltered, devoid of features likely to attract the attention of the compilers of guidebooks, and unremarkable in terms of architecture, scenery or historical and literary associations. For reasons of physical geography, land use, social structure or the pattern of communications, these districts have been to some degree protected from the winds of change, which, although they may have swept, have not in every case swept clean. The traveller may come across them quite unexpectedly, struck by an indefinable change in the scale and quality of the landscape. One category comprises squatter settlements ... The chaotic morphology, with altered and patched-up cottages (originally made of turf and branches) linked by narrow lanes twisting between the irregular enclosures of the smallholding clearly reflects their haphazard origins. Patterns of life such as these, based upon dual economies, have shown themselves in some cases to be remarkably resistant to change. The traditional landscape

forms associated with encroachments still persist in
several districts around the country, bound up with
distinctive local cultures. Their very locations – on the
edge of heaths, moors or forests, beyond the limits of
manorial control or the areas affected by enclosure – have
aided their survival, except where the population has now
declined altogether for want of employment. Even in
instances where, although the cottages are still inhabited,
occupations have changed, the remnants of the old
economies refuse to pass away, as the landscapes
themselves demonstrate."

This kind of landscape, I suspect, is much more widely dispersed
than we imagined, and the same authors remind us that "the
displays of the self-important are only one element" in the
countryside we see, and that "others, in many ways more deep-
seated, are furnished by the countless generations of ordinary people
whose centuries of labour have contributed so much to the cultural
landscape". I find this well-put, and it leads us straight back to our
simplified categories of open and close parishes. This concept has
been modified and elaborated in the last few years in interesting
ways.

I suspect that there are the same complexities about many of the
other things we take for granted from our history lessons, precisely
because of big regional differences which invalidate generalisations.
These include the Welsh *tai unnos*, or One-Night Houses, and the
function of the village tradition of 'Beating the Bounds' at
Rogationtide. Was it a means of resisting enclosures by large landowners, or of reciting encroachments by the landless poor?

The geographer Brian Short in his book *The English Rural
Community*, provides a diagram linking the structure of open and
close parishes, with housing, employment, religion, politics and self-
governing village organisations.

I find the links that this diagram suggests marvellously interesting.
Of course Brian Short hastens to warn us that "in practice, and upon
more detailed investigation, it becomes difficult to categorise
parishes as either 'open' or 'close'. They will rarely approach the
'ideal type' and might instead be placed somewhere along a
continuum." We could talk about the suggested links all afternoon,

but let me mention just two of them. The reference to dual occupations and labourers who were part-time farmers in the open-type village is a reminder of Mike Reed, asking the question "Had the peasantry disappeared in nineteenth century England?" He cites the statement of Eric Hobsbawm that "England was a country of mainly large landlords, cultivated by tenant farmers, working the land with hired labourers", and then goes on to modify this stereotype, pointing out that "Since the census only asked those persons returning themselves as 'farmers' to give details of land held, it gives virtually no information about landholding by people in other occupations."

There were in other words a lot of people who scraped a living in several, probably seasonal occupations including cultivating their own patch.

I should mention the book on *The Making of the Industrial Landscape* by Barrie Trinder. The title of his chapter on squatter settlements is, appropriately, 'A Landscape of Busyness', and the best-known and most visited of squatter cottages is in his area, the one carefully re-erected by the Ironbridge Gorge Museum Trust in Shropshire, with sandstone walls, timber roof construction and (originally) a floor of beaten clay. There Sylvia Bird sits with the cat on her lap, making traditional shopping bags and explaining to us the history of squatters and asks us to imagine how a family of nine lived there in 1861. Barrie Trinder remarks that the cottage at Blists Hill is a "particularly crudely built" example, but of course it had to be, for didactic purposes. Usually there was an evolution over time into a 'normal' house, as extensive as any other home of the period. Precisely the same evolution is seen in the plotland bungalows of the early twentieth century or, in favourable circumstances, in the vast squatter settlements or *barrios* of the later twentieth century around every city in Latin America.

Another well-known squatter cottage where, thanks to photography, evolution can be traced over more than a century, is Jolly Lane Cot near Hexworthy in Devon. William Crossing in his *A Hundred Years on Dartmoor* gives a variant on the sunset to sunrise legend. He says that the belief was that "if a house could be erected and a piece of land enclosed in a single day between sunrise and sunset, the builder could claim such as his own". He goes on to explain that:

"The last instance of such a proceeding occurred about 1835, when a small house now known as Jolly Lane Cot, was built by the side of the road leading to Hexworthy Bridge, on the West Dart. Everything being in readiness, the labourers of the neighbourhood met on the site, on a day when the farmers, who, as holders of the ancient tenements, had rights on the Forest, and would, it was feared, have prevented their plans, had departed to attend Ashburton Fair. Work was commenced, all cheerfully lending assistance. Even before the walls at one end of the house were up, the laying of the thatch of the roof had begun at the other. By evening all was done, and the 'squatters' were in possession. But this attempt at 'land cribbing' was only partially successful. It is true no ejectment followed, but a small rental was put upon the place by the Duchy. The cottage was inhabited until her death in March 1901 by Sally Satterley, the aged widow of its erector, who built it in order to provide a home for his parents."

Her house is there to this day, with another storey added. Mrs Satterley had many of the characteristics of the builders of informal settlements today. One was versatility in undertaking every kind of work. William Crossing wrote admiringly after her death that she, "was during the greater part of her life engaged in work usually performed by men. She was for some time employed in the mine at Eylesbarrow, drove pack-horses, could cut peat, was able to mow with a scythe, and as the father of the present Mr Aaron Rowe, of the Duchy Hotel, Princeton, used to say, could nail a shoe to a horse's hoof as well as a blacksmith."

She was not, in fact, the last of the squatters. More typical were settlements on the fringe of towns, serving the industries concerned with their growth, expansion and servicing in the nineteenth century. Headington Quarry, just outside Oxford, was one of the few such settlements whose story was gathered from survivors before it disappeared in the usual suburban expansion.

The historian Raphael Samuel had been in time to record the memories of local people before they had died and before the anarchic economy and settlement pattern had been expunged from the landscape. His work is set down in his essay 'Quarry roughs: life and labour in Headington Quarry 1860-1920' in R. Samuel's *Village Life and Labour* (Routledge & Kegan Paul, 1975).

He provided a careful link between oral recollections and archives which reveals a community of squatters, working in the quarries and the small brickworks that provided the building materials for nineteenth century Oxford, and which took in its washing. Most cities in Victorian Britain had these service settlements beyond their fringe, like say Notting Dale servicing Notting Hill and Kensington in London, or as Samuel points out, Kensal New Town ('Soapsuds Island') for the fashionable districts of Bayswater and Belgravia, as "chief recipient for the weekly washings of the rich".

This is precisely a function of the 'cities of the poor' in the southern hemisphere today, but Headington Quarry was favoured as a source for both building materials and building techniques. It had both stone and clay, and skills to meet the city's demands, and these, with the equivocal legal ownership of land led to house building and the sharing-out of constructional skills. At the same time it enabled an endless series of poaching, rabbit-snaring, pig-rearing and cow-keeping activities. Every family had an allotment garden and used an incredible series of gathering techniques to exchange within the community or to sell to the farmers or the city. The importance of the vast variety of activities was that, however poor, Quarry people stayed alive outside the official system of poor relief. Raphael Samuel records that:

> "The notion of common rights was built in to the cottager's economy, and so too was that of personal independence: it was possible to make 'a bit of a living' even when wage-paid labour gave out, and even when there was no money, to keep the table supplied with food, and have enough fuel to feed the fire. Perhaps it is this which helps to explain why Quarry, though 'rough' by the standards of more regulated communities, seems to have escaped the kind of destitution so familiar in the late Victorian countryside, and so rampant in the towns. Subsistence never gave out, however severe the season, nor was charity ever called upon to take its place – there

was little available save that which the working
population of the village provided for themselves."

And he points to the fact that in neither the official census returns
nor in the recollections he gathered from old villagers, "in all the
hardships which they speak about" is any mention made "of those
two great standbys of the out-of-work elsewhere: the workhouse and
parish relief".

In the context of the history of the English poor, living outside
these hated and feared institutions was a remarkable achievement,
and it was also, as Raphael Samuel noted, a village which had arisen
singularly free of landlords. "For centuries it had enjoyed what was
virtually an extra-parochial existence, a kind of anarchy, in which the
villagers were responsible to nobody but themselves."

For any student of the informal economy in the squatter
settlements of the southern hemisphere today, and of the
relationships and connection between the official, GNP-included
economy and the unofficial sector that actually keeps people alive,
Raphael Samuel's essay in oral history at Headington Quarry is
fascinating.

The Quarry was outside the stereotyped economy of wage labour
and capital. He notes how:

> "Numbers of villagers escaped the servitudes of wage
> labour altogether, and there were many more for whom
> employment was characteristically short term and
> indirect. Within the village nothing like a capitalist class
> emerged. In building the smaller jobs were often taken on
> by pairs of mates, or by individuals acting on their own,
> or with a helper. Stone-digging work and navvying were
> often in the hands of 'companionships' – self-selecting
> bands of men, linked to one another by ties of friendship
> or blood and sometimes both."

I mentioned how 'women's work' was, overwhelmingly, washing
clothes for the colleges, chapels and posh houses of Oxford, and this
of course had a sub-trade in delivery boys, carriers' carts and even
laundry-basket making. In the 'male trades', stone had been
quarried there since the fifteenth century, so there were both quarry

and masons, as well as innumerable humbler work associated with stone, from cobbles for street paving and the rubble stone from which houses in and out of Quarry were built. But there was also clay for brickmaking, which stayed a family activity. Samuel notes that "No dynasty of brickmakers appeared, even in the heyday of the industry's local prosperity, nor was there a decisive separation of wage labour and capital". In the whole range of the building trades, there was a "bias towards rough, open-air work".

At the same time it was a rural place, so there was subsistence farming, horticulture and the universal world of allotment-gardening, pig-keeping, poultry-rearing, poaching, and gleaning fuel and much else from the woods. Everything had a market, from rabbits to leaf-mould and moss, and holly berries, sold to the florist's shops of Oxford.

Headington Quarry was, in living memory, when Raphael Samuel collected the recollections of old people, a precise parallel to the 'cities of the poor' in much of the world today. One of my own ambitions is, some day, to write a book about the geographical distribution of the folklore about the houses built in one night (or one day) which is to be found all over the Celtic fringe of Britain as well as further east, in Brittany, in the Basque provinces of southern France and northern Spain, and hence in the New World, and to link this with the accumulation we have of local studies in this country.

I have named the ones I know about in my list of sources, in the hope that people here will tell me of others that *they* know about. Please give me your point of view. Next week I propose to talk about those informal settlements that town-planners call the 'plotlands' from the first forty years of the twentieth century.

References and Sources

General

Paul Coones and John Patten (1986) *The Penguin Guide to the Landscape of England and Wales*, Penguin Books.

Brian Short (Ed.) (1992) *The English Rural Community: Image and Reality*, Cambridge University Press.

Mark Overton (1986) *Agricultural Revolution? England 1540-1850*, ReFRESH – Recent Findings of Research in Economic and Social History, No. 3, Autumn.

Barrie Trinder (1982) *The Making of the Industrial Landscape*, J.M. Dent (Alan Sutton, 1987).

J.L. and Barbara Hammond (1911) *The Village Labourer*, Guild Books (1949).

Colin Ward (1980) 'The Early Squatters' in Nick Wates (Ed.) *Squatting: The Real Story*, Bay Leaf Books.

Mick Reed (1984) 'The Peasantry of Nineteenth-Century England: a neglected class?', *History Workshop*, No. 18, Autumn.

Mick Reed (1986) 'Nineteenth-century rural England: a case for peasant studies?', *Journal of Peasant Studies*, 14 (1).

Case Histories

Chris Fisher (1978) 'The Free Miners of the Forest of Dean 1800-1841' in Royden Harrison (Ed.) *The Independent Collier: The Coal Miner as Archetypal Proletarian Reconsidered*, Harvester Press.

Graham Rogers (1993) 'Custom and Common Right: Waste Land Enclosure and Social Change in West Lancashire' in *Agricultural History Review*, Vol. 41, Part II.

James Moir (1990) 'A World Unto Themselves? Squatter Settlement in Herefordshire 1780-1880' (Unpublished PhD Thesis, University of Leicester).

Eurwyn Wiliam (1993) *Home-made Homes: Dwellings of the rural poor in Wales*, National Museum of Wales.

Andrew Dobraszcxyc (1993) *A Walk around Baddeley Edge* and *A Walk around Mow Cop*, Stoke-on-Trent: West Mercia Workers Educational Association.

Crispin Paine and John Rhodes (1979) *The Worker's Home: Small Houses in Oxfordshire Through Three Centuries*, Oxfordshire Museum Service, Publication No. 10.

Ken Jones, Maurice Hunt, John Malam and Barrie Trinder (1982) 'Holywell Lane: A squatter community in the Shropshire Coalfield', *Industrial Archaeology Review*, Vol. VI, No. 3, Autumn.

Raphael Samuel (1975) 'Quarry Roughs: Life and labour in Headington Quarry, 1860-1920 – an essay in oral history' in Raphael Samuel (Ed.) *Village Life and Labour*, Routledge & Kegan Paul.

William Crossing (1901) *A Hundred Years on Dartmoor*, Western Morning News (David and Charles, 1967).

William Crossing (1912) *Crossing's Guide to Dartmoor*, (David and Charles, 1965).

Principles
John Turner (1976) *Housing By People: Towards Autonomy in Building Environments*, Marion Boyars: London (Pantheon Books: New York, 1977).

2. The plotlanders: arcadians of the early twentieth century

Last week I took a very brief look at the history of squatter settlement in Britain before the twentieth century. Today I turn to the plotlands of the first forty years of this century. The word 'plotlands' was coined by planners for those places where, until 1939, land was divided into small plots and sold, often in unorthodox ways, to people wanting to build their holiday home, country retreat or would-be smallholding. It evokes a landscape of a grid-iron of grassy tracks, sparsely filled with bungalows made from army huts, old railway coaches, sheds, shanties and chalets, slowly evolving into ordinary suburban development.

By 1939 this plotland landscape was to be found in pockets across the North Downs, along the Hampshire plain, and in the Thames Valley at riverside sites like Penton Hook, Marlow Bottom and Purley Park. It was interspersed among the established holiday resorts on the coasts of East and West Sussex at places like Shoreham Beach, Pett Level, Dungeness and Camber Sands, and most notoriously of all, at Peacehaven. It crept up the east coast, from Sheppey in Kent to Lincolnshire, by way of Canvey Island and Jaywick Sands, and clustered in land all across south Essex.

The plotlands were the result of several factors. First, the agricultural decline that began in the 1870s and continued until 1939, with a break in the First World War, forced the sale of bankrupt farms at throw-away prices. Also the break-up of landed estates after Lloyd George's doubling of death duties, coupled with the slaughter of sons and heirs in Flanders, added to the pressure among sellers of land to find a multitude of small buyers in the absence of a few large ones.

Added to this was the spread down the social scale of the holiday habit and the 'weekend' idea. The Holidays With Pay Act of 1938 affected eighteen and a half million employed workers, nearly eleven million of whom were to receive holiday pay for the first time. Those who had previously taken a holiday without being paid for that week or fortnight were likely to seek a cheap one, and a glance at *Dalton's Weekly* in the 1930s showed that the cheapest holiday available was to rent a plotland bungalow. The availability of cheap transport was also important, as was the cult of the great outdoors.

Finally there was the idea of a property-owning democracy. The owner-occupied house is now the commonest mode of tenure in this country, and even when most families, rich or poor, rented their dwellings, the attraction of possessing a few square yards of England had its appeal. Long before a minor Conservative politician coined the phrase about property-owning, one plotland entrepreneur, Frederick Francis Ramus of Southend, who operated as The Land Company, was advertising in 1906 that 'Land nationalisation is coming', meaning that the dominance of the absentee landlord would be replaced by every family owning its own portion of our common birthright.

The plotlands have several characteristics in common. They were invariably on marginal land. The Essex plotlands were on the heavy clay known to farmers as three-horse land, which was the first to go out of cultivation in the agricultural depression. Others grew up on vulnerable coastal sites like Jaywick Sands and Canvey Island, or on estuary marshland or riverside sites like those in the Thames Valley which are also liable to flooding, or they are on acid heathland or chalky uplands.

Another characteristic is that the plotlanders wanted their holiday homes to stay in the same family and eventually to become the owners' retirement home. What seemed to the outside observer to be inconvenient, substandard and far from the shops, was for them loaded with memories of happy summer days when the children were small.

Finally, the plotlands tended, unless deliberate obstacles were put in the residents' way (as they quite often were) to be upgraded over time. Extensions, the addition of bathrooms, partial or total rebuilding, the provision of mains services and the making-up of roads are part of the continuous improvement process in any old settlement that has not been economically undermined or subjected to the restraint on improvements known as planners' blight.

The nineteenth century saw the mushroom growth of British cities. The twentieth century has seen an irresistible pressure from city dwellers, once they had any freedom of choice, to get out again. Hence the immense growth of leapfrogging suburbs, and the development of 'out-county' estates provided by city authorities taking advantage of the availability of cheap land outside their own boundaries.

The political response to this enormous outward movement was all-party support for restriction of ribbon development, for Green Belts and New Towns, and for the development-control system of planning that has existed since the Second World War, as well as the growth of amenity and conservation pressure groups seeking to preserve the countryside against further incursion.

The pre-war literature of planning and conservation reveals the intense horror felt by all 'right-thinking' (that is, privileged) people at the desecration of the landscape that was happening everywhere. Dean Inge, a celebrated publicist of the period, coined the phrase 'bungaloid growth' with its implication that some kind of cancer was creeping over the face of the Home Counties. Howard Marshall, in the compendium *Britain and the Beast*, published in 1937, declared that "a gimcrack civilisation crawls like a giant slug over the country, leaving a foul trail of slime behind it". It is hard not to feel in retrospect that part of this disgust was ordinary misanthropy – the wrong sort of people were getting a place in the sun.

Of all new developments the plotlands were the most vulnerable. They seldom complied with the building by-laws, it was argued that they were a menace to public health, their rateable value was very low, and their owners were not people with an influential voice in public affairs. When raw and new they looked more like the fringes of boom towns, springing up in a grid-iron of dirt roads as in the American West or the Australian bush, than the pattern of urban growth expected in south-east England.

But there is an irony in the fact that the simple life and the rural weekend also attracted the liberal intelligentsia who were the backbone of the preservationist lobby. Reginald Bray was a progressive philanthropist who left London in 1919 to administer his father's estates at Shere, near Guildford in Surrey. The estate papers were studied in the 1980s by Dr Peter Brandon who finds that Bray provided sites for weekend cottages on the estate for many of the good and the great of the period, including most of the members of the first Labour Cabinet and founders of the London School of Economics. Among the weekend residents were several crusaders for the protection of the countryside. They included Clough Williams-Ellis, who later built the delightful make-believe holiday village of Portmeirion, and who wrote *England and the Octopus* and who edited *Britain and the Beast*.

He deplored the way in which "the adventurous bungalow plants its foundations – a pink asbestos roof screaming its challenge – across a whole parish from some pleasant upland that it light-heartedly defaced". Another of the weekend residents in Surrey was Bray's fellow Harrovian, the historian G.M. Trevelyan, who lamented that, as he put it, "the State is socialist enough to destroy by taxation the classes that used to preserve rural amenity, but is still too conservative to interfere in the purposes to which land is put by speculators to whom the land is sold".

By the 1990s we surely find something unattractive about the way the shapers of policy took it for granted that *they* were entitled to a country retreat while wanting to deny, on aesthetic grounds, the same opportunity to people further down the hierarchy of income and opportunity. In any case, time and nature have changed the plot-land sites just as they have changed any raw new settlement. For example, those offending salmon-pink asbestos-cement slates have, besides proving to be as durable as other roofing materials, attracted moss and lichen so that their appearance is like that of Cotswold stone.

In the post-war decades, what have planning authorities done about the plotlands? Sometimes their aim was to eliminate them totally and return the land, if not to agriculture, to public recreational use. In most places this policy has failed and resulted in empty scrubby wasteland between those plots still occupied by obstinate people who fought planning decisions, with the result that local planning authorities were overruled by central government. In some places it has succeeded. At Havering Park, Essex, the Greater London Council bought and demolished all plotland dwellings to make a country park. Nearby, the new town of Basildon was designated in 1949 to make some kind of urban entity out of Pitsea and Laindon, where by the end of the war there was a settled population of about 25,000 served by 75 miles of grass-track roads, mostly with no sewers and with standpipes for water supply. More recently Essex County Council eliminated another scattered plotland areas to make the new residential town of South Woodham Ferrers.

When Dennis Hardy and I were funded by the then Social Science Research Council to do our plotland research, we confined ourselves to the south-east of England and the London hinterland. This was as much as we could handle and we had both been studying these settlements for years. But the plotland phenomenon wasn't confined to the south-east. Every industrial conurbation in Britain once had these escape routes to the country, river or sea. For the West Midlands there was the Severn Valley or North Wales, for Liverpool and Manchester, places in the Wirral, for Glasgow the Ayrshire coast and even the banks of Loch Lomond, for the West Riding towns and cities, the Yorkshire coast and the Humber estuary, and for those of Tyneside and Teesside, the coasts of Northumberland and Durham. It is as though a proportion of the population were obeying a law of nature in seeking out a place where they could build for themselves.

Anybody familiar with the aspirations of city dwellers in the former Soviet Union or of its Empire – countries like Poland, Hungary, Czechoslovakia or Bulgaria, will be thoroughly familiar with this aspiration for a little patch out of town which evolves from an allotment to a second home and ultimately to *the* family *dacha* and home base.

Attitudes towards the plotlands have changed over the years. They began as a blot on the landscape. Then they were seen as odd, curious or vaguely interesting or quaint. After that, inevitably, they were perceived as a precious aspect of our Heritage. At Basildon, one of the few remaining bungalows called The Haven at Dunton Hills became a plotland museum. At Dungeness in Kent, a plotland site was designated as a Conservation Area in order to preserve it from redevelopment. Even the antiquated railway carriages that people bought for £15 each, delivered by horse-drawn transport to the site, have become precious for the railway antiquarians.

You will probably have heard during the past year of the efforts to save a plotland site called Holt's Field in Swansea Bay. Since 1934 the people who built their chalets there have paid a nominal annual licence fee to their landlords, the Holt family. But the new landlords are a property company seeing the site as having a development value of £2 to £3 million, and they sought to get rid of the 27 chalet owners. Swansea Council refused planning permission to the developer, declaring the site to be 'arcadian' and designating it a Conservation Area in 1990, even though the council's environmental health officers felt obliged to declare many of the homes as unfit for habitation. The case is still meandering through the courts.

When Dennis Hardy and I were enabled to explore the plotlands, while plenty of the original settlers were still living, what struck us, just as it has struck people interviewing the residents of Holt's Field today, was their enormous attachment to their homes, their defensive independence and their strong community bonds. The residents of Jaywick Sands, for example, had for decades organised a service for emptying Elsan closets, known locally as the Bisto Kids, until, after fifty years, a sewer was built. Our overwhelming impression was of the way that the plotland self-builders, who started with very little, over the years turned their own labour and ingenuity into capital, with no help at all from building societies, local councils or any other financial institutions. Take, for example, the following two case histories.

Fred Nichols of Bowers Gifford in Essex, was in his late seventies when we met him 25 years ago. He had a poverty-stricken childhood in East London and a hard and uncertain life as a casual dock labourer. His plot, twelve metres wide and thirty metres deep, cost him £10 in 1934. To begin with he put up a tent, which his family and friends used at weekends, and he gradually accumulated tools, timber and glass which he brought to the site strapped to his back as he cycled the 25 miles from London. For water, he sank a well in his garden. His house was called Perseverance.

Mrs Sayers had lived at Peacehaven since 1923. Her husband, severely wounded in the First World War, was urged to live in a more bracing, upland climate than that of London. They applied to estate agents in the Surrey Hills but found houses there far beyond their reach. After reading about Peacehaven in the publicity printed on the backs of London tram tickets by the flamboyant speculator who started that settlement, they bought three adjacent plots at £50 each. They got the land in 1921, built on it in 1923, opened a branch post office and grocery store and lived there happily for many decades.

My typical plotlander was Elizabeth Grainger who wrote to me after hearing me talking about this topic on the Jimmy Young show on the radio. When I went to see her she poured out her autobiography with the tea. She paid the deposit on her £5 plot with a borrowed pound, and her final remark to me was that "I feel so sorry for young people these days. They don't get the opportunities we had".

The same kind of aspirations still exist, as we can see from the 'leisure plots' racket which arise every few years, where speculators sell plots without planning permission to gullible purchasers who discover that there is nothing they can legally do with their blessed plots. The conservation lobby is horrified at the suggestion that such sites should be selectively licensed. Most of us would readily agree that some of the inter-war plotland sites should never have been built on, simply because of flood danger. But most of them are so obscure and hidden that the ordinary explorer like me gets lost looking for them, and has to make a special journey in order to be affronted. Not all land is so precious that it must be devoted to raising the European grain mountain, or more likely to be set aside to produce nothing at the public expense. Not all principles of planning are so precious that they cannot be ignored a little, here and there.

The Second World War and the overwhelming powers to control development given to planning authorities by the 1947 Town and Country Planning Act and its successors put an end to this kind of self-help house-building in Britain. Even self-build housing, which provides more home annually today than any of the multiple 'volume house-builders', has to produce a fully-finished, fully-serviced house right from the start. Otherwise there is no planning permission, no approval under the Building Regulations and no mortgage loan to pay for the site and materials. Other countries have room for opportunities for the would-be home-builder who starts with nothing and turns labour into capital over time.

At first sight it seems absurd to compare the English plotlands of the first half of this century with the explosion of self-built informal settlements that surround every Third World city in the second half. In the English example it was a marginal phenomenon, whereas in the cities of Latin America, Africa and Asia, the unofficial self-housed inhabitants outnumber those of the official cities. But our investigation of the plotlanders and the homes they made for themselves reminded us continually of the findings of those investigators of Third World self-built settlements who see them as triumphs of popular initiative and ingenuity. For example, twenty years ago John Turner and Bryan Roberts concluded that:

> "ordinary people use resources and opportunities available to them with imagination and initiative – when

they have access to the necessary resources, and when
they are free to act for themselves. Anyone who can see
beyond the many forms of dwelling place people build for
themselves is bound to be struck by the often astonishing
economy of housing built and managed locally, or from
the bottom up, in comparison with top-down, mass
housing, supplied by large organisations and central
agencies."

Everything that we learned from the plotlanders confirms this
interpretation, but I need to mention another observation on the
plotland phenomenon. While Dennis Hardy and I were gathering
from survivors the evolution of the plotlands, another researcher,
Anthony King, in his monumental, global history of the bungalow as
a building type, drew a significant conclusion from these places and
the circumstances that linked them with the ancient tradition of
squatter housing, and made possible this twentieth century
equivalent. He remarked that:

"A combination of cheap land and transport, pre-
fabricated materials, and the owner's labour and skills
had given back, to the ordinary people of the land, the
opportunity denied to them for over two hundred years,
an opportunity which, at the time, was still available to
almost half of the world's non-industrialised population:
the freedom for a man to build his own house. It was a
freedom that was to be very short-lived."

This comment leads us straight back to last week's seminar on
cotters and squatters in English history and to our exploration next
week of the lessons to be gathered from the post-war squatters'
movements.

References and Sources

Dennis Hardy and Colin Ward (1984) *Arcadia for All: the legacy of a makeshift landscape*, Mansell.

Mark Irving (1995) 'A Doomed Arcadia' in *Perspectives on Architecture*, September.

John Turner and Bryan Roberts (1975) 'The self-help society' in Peter Wilsher and Rosemary Righter (Eds.) *The Exploding Cities*, Andre Deutsch.

Anthony King (1984) *The Bungalow: A global history*, Routledge and Kegan Paul.

3. Learning from post-war squatters' movements

In the first of these seminars I looked at historical aspects of settlement on common or waste land and in the second at the purchase of land at throw-away prices during the agricultural depression that lasted until the second world war. But in the post-war decades the word 'squatting' has been used to describe the unauthorised occupation of empty property (almost invariably publicly-owned) by homeless people.

It seems to me that squatting can be seen as *ideological* or *pragmatic*. What I mean by this is that when Winstanley and the Diggers settled on land at Walton-on-Thames in Surrey in 1649, they were ideologists, dramatising a century of unauthorised encroachments, pushed on as Christopher Hill noted, "by land shortage and pressure of population". Similarly, when in September 1969 squatters occupied a former royal residence, No. 144 Piccadilly in central London, with a banner proclaiming Proudhon's slogan 'Property is Theft', they were ideologists, dramatising the scandal of homelessness in a city where at the time acres of useable housing was empty, waiting for vast redevelopment proposals and road-building, which in the event never happened. We need to be reminded of the finding by Dr Graham Lomas that in London by 1975, more fit houses had been destroyed than had been built since the Second World War.

There have always been pragmatic squatters, relying on the distant and absentee property-owners, to allow them the occupation of premises by default. The last thing they desired was publicity and the thing they most desired was a rent-book and security of tenure. You will know that the term 'Squatters' Rights' is a popular term for the complicated case-law of Adverse Possession, which means, broadly-speaking, that if you have had unchallenged occupation of land or buildings for twelve years, you can claim ownership.

We have a continuous history of squatting in the margins of history. A Victorian historian of Windsor Castle observed that at one time paupers had squatted in many of the towers. In the early nineteenth century an apple seller called Ann Hicks annexed a portion of Hyde Park at the east end of the Serpentine. Her shanty was known as the

White House and was steadily improved. An admirer, Katherine
Lloyd, explained that:

> "From a stall with an awning, a lock-up shop was
> evolved. Then a small back enclosure appeared including
> four walls with windows and a door. The height of the
> building was next increased, and under the excuse of
> repairing the roof a chimney was provided. The next step
> was to get a hurdle erected to prevent the curious from
> peeping in at the window. The fence by degrees was moved
> outwards, until a fair amount of space was enclosed. At
> this stage the authorities intervened and secured
> possession of the domain of Ann Hicks who was granted
> a small allowance."

However, I have to turn to the period at the end of the Second World
War. It started in 1945 with what was known as the Vigilante
campaign which spread from Brighton to other seaside towns like
Hastings and Southend. Committees of, largely, ex-servicemen,
under cover of night, installed homeless families and their furniture
in unoccupied houses – usually successfully, since no action could be
taken to evict them once they were in, until the usually absentee
property-owners could initiate legal proceedings against them.

   In the following year the campaign grew because of the anomaly of
the emptying-out of hundreds of army and air force camps during
the worst housing shortage the country had known. The first of the
1946 squatters was James Fielding, a cinema projectionist from
Scunthorpe who, desperate for somewhere to live so that he could
keep his job, moved on 8th May with his family, into the former
officers' mess of an unoccupied anti-aircraft camp. As soon as the
news of their action spread around the town, other young couples in
a similar predicament moved into the other huts and the first of the
new squatter colonies was born. Two other camps in Lincolnshire
were seized, and this was followed by the occupation of several camps
around Sheffield. At Sheffield settlers formed a Squatters' Protection
Society and linked up with the pioneer squatters at Scunthorpe.

   These events were rapidly followed by the seizure of hundred of
camps everywhere in Britain. The authorities who at first disclaimed
any responsibility for the squatters – passing the buck from one

department to another – were forced to recognise the occupations, and local authorities were instructed to turn on water and electricity supplies. Later in the year the Ministry of Works, which had previously declared itself 'not interested' found it possible to offer the Ministry of Health (then the department responsible for housing) 850 former service camps.

The government announced on 11th October 1946 that 1,038 camps in England and Wales had been occupied by 39,535 people, and on 5th September it was stated that four thousand people had squatted in Scotland. Since the government could not destroy the movement, it tried to absorb it, and expressed itself confident that the settlers would "see reason" and "move out when the situation had been explained to them". On Saturday 14th September, the Minister of Health, Aneurin Bevan, just back from his holiday in Switzerland, instructed local authorities to cut off gas and electricity supplies to property under their control occupied by squatters.

But in fact, by this time, councils were already directing homeless people to occupy empty huts where by this time settlers were organising communal cooking and nursery facilities and forming a rota to stoke the boilers left behind by the armed forces. A very revealing report in a series called 'How Are They Now?' appeared in the *News Chronicle* for 14th January 1947. The correspondent described a Lancashire camp:

> "There are two camps within the camp – the official squatters (that is, people who have been placed in the huts after the first invasion) and the unofficial squatters (the veterans who have been allowed to remain on sufferance). Both pay the same rent of ten shillings a week – but there the similarity ends. Although one would have imagined that the acceptance of rent form both should accord them identical privileges, in fact it does not. Workmen have put up partitions in the huts of the official squatters and have put in sinks and numerous other conveniences. These are the sheep; the goats have perforce to fend for themselves.

An interesting commentary on the situation was made by one of the young welfare officers attached to the housing department. On her visit of inspection she found that the goats had set to work with a will, improvising partitions, running up curtains, distempering, painting and using initiative. The official squatters on the other hand, sat about glumly without lifting a hand to help themselves and bemoaning their fate, even though they might have been removed from the most appalling slum property. Until the overworked corporation workmen got around to them they would not attempt to improve affairs themselves."

In October 1946, Aneurin Bevan sought to turn public feeling against the camp squatters by suggesting that they were "jumping their place in the housing queue", when in fact they were jumping out of the housing queue by moving into buildings which would not otherwise have been used for housing purposes. It took most of them years in fact to get into that "housing queue". Over a hundred families who in 1946 occupied a camp called Field Farm in Oxfordshire, stayed together and over ten years later in 1958-9 were rehoused in the new village of Berinsfield on the same site.

But meanwhile, as the camps began to fill, squatters turned to other empty buildings: houses, shops, mansions, disused school buildings, race tracks and a stadium were among the places occupied, and on 26th August 1946 two Aberdeen hotels and on the 29th two big Glasgow hotels were seized, and later abandoned. The final and most spectacular phase of the campaign began in London on Sunday 8th September when the 148 former luxury flats of Duchess of Bedford House, Kensington, another block in Weymouth Street, Marylebone, and big empty houses in Holland Park and Camden Hill were occupied. On the following day three more houses in Marylebone were taken over, and on the Tuesday sixty families entered Fountain Court, a block of flats in Victoria. On Wednesday the flats at Abbey Lodge, Regents Park and the 630-room Ivanhoe Hotel in Bloomsbury were occupied. The tactics adopted by the police varied from day to day, from sympathy to threats, according to instructions from above.

The Communist Party, although a year earlier it had denounced the Brighton Vigilantes, was very active among the London squatters. So much so that people who had to rely on newspapers for their information assumed, and have assumed since, that the whole thing was a Communist stunt. The whole affair ended in the anti-climax of a 'general evacuation' by the London squatters when a

High Court injunction against them was granted. This was seen as the end of the squatting wave, though many of them were found accommodation of one kind or another by the London County Council, while the camp squatters had settled down until they could find something better.

Needless to say, pragmatic squatting continued, especially as local councils acquired vast tracts of urban housing for eventual comprehensive redevelopment. It re-emerged as a public issue in 1968 thanks to two activists, Ron Bailey and Jim Radford. They were busy agitating about the failure of local authorities to comply with their statutory duty to the homeless, trying after long and bitter campaigns to draw public attention to conditions in hostels for homeless families in Kent and Essex and in the LCC area. By this time, as Bailey put it, "a squatting campaign was clearly on the cards; it only needed a spark to set it off", so they installed homeless families in unoccupied houses which had been publicly acquired and earmarked for demolition years later for eventual road improvements, car parking or municipal offices.

This outraged the local authorities who responded violently. They used thugs described as 'private investigators' as their agents to terrorise and intimidate the squatting families, and this was widely reported and photographed in the press and on television, and this in turn drew public opinion towards support of the squatters, as did the policy of deliberately wrecking the interiors of empty houses just to keep the squatters out. I myself saw the way in which council employees smashed sinks and water closets, poured cement down the wastepipes and ripped out staircases so that even squatters could not settle there.

Bailey was commissioned by Penguin Books to write his account of the events in 1969, but his book was not published until 1973 because of lawsuits resulting from the activities of the so-called 'bailiffs' employed by one London council. When it did appear, his publishers omitted his concluding chapter which defended the squatters' movement both against those who oppose direct action from a constitutional point of view, and secondly against his critics on the allegedly revolutionary left. He remarked that:

> "In the squatters' movement I have worked with ordinary
> non-political people for admittedly small gains, and we

achieved a large measure of success. Ordinary people
acted and won; and ordinary people manage the houses
in which they now live. So when councils offered to hand
over houses we accepted these rather than fight over them
unnecessarily" (Ron Bailey, 'In Defence of Direct Action'
in *Wildcat* No. 3, November 1974).

For what happened after the grotesque over-reaction of councils to
the activities of the squatters, was that, ashamed of their
mismanagement of empty housing they owned, they gladly entered
into agreements for short-life housing co-ops, some of which,
because of the changed climate of housing policy, have had a very
long life. In London, some of the most successful housing co-ops
have grown out of squatting groups. And in fact, a quarter of a
century after his venture into the squatting world, Bailey dedicates
his most recent book on the scandal of empty housing in a situation
of homelessness, to the late Conservative chairman of the housing
committee of the London Borough of Lewisham in 1968-71, in
"admiration of the astonishing courage and vision he showed by
entering into the first legal agreement with squatters in 1969" and
he adds that "as a result of his election, tens of thousands of homes
that would otherwise have stayed empty have been brought back into
use and hundreds of thousands of homeless people given new hope
and dignity".

Local politicians may have come to agreements with squatters (and
this is perhaps more evident in other European cities like
Amsterdam and Copenhagen), but central government politicians of
both major parties have been unremittingly hostile. Once they
discovered that squatting was a civil, rather than a criminal offence,
governed by legislation dating back to the year 1381, they set about
changing the situation. The Law Commission responded in 1974
with a document on Criminal Law Offences of Entering and
Remaining on Property, which was incorporated into legislation by
the Criminal Law Act of 1977. This failed to deter this country's
50,000 or so squatters, and in practice, so has its Conservative
successor, the infamous Criminal Justice Act of 1994.

During the preparation of the Labour government's legislation,
surveys of squatters were undertaken by Mike Kingham and others,
which demonstrated that typical squatters were not happy hippies,

but people in desperate housing need. In preparation for the Criminal Justice Act twenty years later, the Home Office issued a Consultation Paper in which it stated that it "does not accept the claim that squatting results from social deprivation. Squatters are generally there by their own choice, moved by no more than self-gratification or an unreadiness to respect other people's rights" (paragraph 62). It also observed that cases of squatting 'involving very young children were negligible" (paragraph 9).

Ron Bailey in his most recent book uses the latest available survey figures to show that the facts are very different. He finds that:

> "About one third of squatting households contain children and this has been the case for over five years. Under Section 58 of the Housing Act 1985, all such families are statutorily homeless and so entitled to be accommodated by local authorities. This would often be bed and breakfast. The fact that they are squatting actually saves ratepayers vast amounts of money. Many other squatters need psychiatric help; since 1990 more than 28,000 hospital beds have been lost and only 5,000 residential places provided. Thus, many ill people have drifted into sleeping rough and squatting. In addition, currently 2,000 squatters are women escaping violent partners. Even more squatters are homeless single people for whom there is no statutory provision at all and for whom council waiting lists are meaningless. About one in twenty squatters (2,500 people) are ex-owner occupiers, evicted as they were unable to meet mortgage repayments. In conclusion, therefore, all the available evidence shows that squatters are homeless people in desperate housing need, often with other social problems such as mental illness or the need to escape violence and harassment. These are the people that the government is attempting to make into criminals."

The government ignored the representations of eminently reasonable people like Ron Bailey who for thirty years has tried, to seek some accommodation for the homeless in official policy, and, as you will know, the Criminal Justice Act incorporated an astonishing ragbag of legislation directed against the poor. I will be returning to this topic next week.

What squatters seek, and have always sought, is security of tenure, and I must add, personal security. In our topsy-turvy economy it is easier to own a lot of expensive consumer goods than to have a secure home and to achieve security for your personal possessions.

What I deplore is that degeneration in the public mood which enabled local authorities in the 1940s or Conservative councillors in the 1960s and 1970s to make creative deals with squatters, but in the 1990s, government, relying for support on what it sees as the self-protective instincts of an allegedly property-owning democracy, has been busy, once again, in the task of criminalising them. I want to pick up this theme in considering the future of unofficial settlements in the last of this group of seminars.

References and Sources

Ron Bailey (1973) *The Squatters*, Penguin Books.

Ron Bailey (1994) *Homelessness: what can be done? An immediate programme of self-help and mutual aid,* John Carpenter Publishing, PO Box 129, Oxford, OX1 4PH.

Diana Murray Hill (1946) 'Who are the squatters?', *Pilot Papers*, November.

James Hinton (1988) 'Self-help and Socialism: The Squatters' movement of 1946', *History Workshop Journal.*

Mike Kingham (1974) 'Tenant self-management – the experience of Family Squatting Associations', *Housing Review*, July-August.

Graham Lomas (1975) *The Inner City*, London Council of Social Service.

Colin Ward (1980) 'The Early Squatters', Nick Wates (Ed.) *Squatting: The Real Story*, Bay Leaf Books.

Colin Ward (1963) 'Direct action for houses: the story of the squatters', *Anarchy*, Vol. 3, No. 1, January (reprinted by the London Squatters, 1969).

Colin Ward (1976) 'What have the squatters achieved?' in *Housing: An Anarchist Approach*, Freedom Press.

4. Travellers and settlers in the 21st century

In the past three weeks we have looked briefly at several kinds of unofficial housing, based on personal and local self-help and mutual aid: the history of rural squatter settlements, the unofficial self-built colonies of the early twentieth century that planners call the 'plotlands' and the post-war squatters' movements. There are other forms of unofficial housing we could consider. One obvious one is that of 'mobile homes', the British equivalent of American 'trailer parks', which are one way of getting round the constraints of the building regulations and winning the tolerance of planning authorities. The pretence is that these are movable dwellings, though they are seldom, once planted on a site, actually moved.

But I need to look today at the future of those people who really are mobile out of choice or necessity. You will know that all through English history there have always been travelling people with an indispensable role in the traditional labour-intensive rural economy in seasonal work at harvest-time, and that even today, when arable farmers aim to do without any permanent labour force, they have a vital place in potato-lifting, fruit-picking, and in hopfields and orchards.

In the eighteenth and nineteenth century there were also the travelling navvies and their families too, who built the canals and the railways, just as there were canal-boat families, fairground families, and dynasties of horse-breeders and traders. Contrary to legend, many adapted to a settled way of life when low-rent housing was available. Others, evicted by the plough-up of those odd pockets of land where they used to camp, and as the demand for traditional gypsy crafts like tin-smithery, clothes-peg-making and similar crafts like broom and basket making died away, changed locations to the urban fringe and adapted to new trades like tarmac-laying and car-breaking.

Conscious that there have been travelling people in these islands for a lot longer than, for example, the royal family, many people have a kind of distant sympathy for them, aware of and ashamed by several recent histories of a tradition of persecution. They may be fascinated, thanks to the new interest in vernacular architecture, in the evolution of the caravans and instant shelters built by gypsies, the Irish tinkers and the Scottish travellers. This interest has tended to evaporate when the gypsies, like everyone else, became motorised.

The planning legislation, allocating an approved use to every patch of land, added to the problems faced by travelling people. It was recognition of these new dilemmas for a minority which as the historian of the gypsies, Angus Fraser remarks, have "clung tenaciously to some ideal of community and independence and self-employment", that led to the passing of the Caravan Sites Act of 1968, which required local councils to provide sites for gypsies with a 100 per cent grant from central government. Less that two-fifths of them actually did and the Act was not enforced.

All the same, the 1968 Act had its importance as a gesture towards civilisation. The fact that the entire cost of providing sites was met by the central budget removed the argument that travellers were a charge to ratepayers, and the fact that the legislation existed was a useful defence when the continued harassment of gypsies was challenged in court by bodies like the National Gypsy Council.

In 1978 the Government asked the late Professor Gerald Wibberley, a much respected authority on countryside planning, to report on the workings of the Act. He concluded that "The Act is working, slowly, but quite well in a few areas, even though councils and government didn't have their heart in it". Then, on 18th August 1992, when Parliament was in recess and just after the grouse-shooting season had begun, with a hoard of well-heeled itinerants descending on moorland areas, Sir George Young, then Minister of State for Housing and Planning, announced his intention to make it a criminal offence to park a caravan or similar vehicle on any land, without the landowner's consent, and to remove the obligation on local authorities to provide sites.

Sir George said, with a straight face, that it was up to travellers to acquire their own land for sites and to apply for planning consent. He denied that abandoning the 1968 Act would bring a return of the terrible scenes (and actual deaths) that caused it: the dawn battles of the 1960s between travelling people and bailiffs employed by local councils, backed up by the police. He also claimed that the Act had failed since only 38% of councils had complied with it, and told Radio 4's reporter that his proposals were not directed at what he called 'genuine gypsies'.

I have no idea how Sir George Young has learned to identify a 'genuine' gypsy, a skill that has always evaded me, but one 61-year-old Romany, Martin Ward, whose family had lived for eighteen years on the council site beneath the Westway flyover in London, told the reporters on the following day that the new legislation amounted to 'ethnic cleansing'.

Precisely the same phrase was used on 27th November 1992 by Professor Wibberley, who said: "It is sad to me that the government have allowed themselves to take an *ethnic cleansing* approach". Sir George Young's proposals were of course incorporated in the Criminal Justice Act of 1994, and there have been test cases which enable us to question his assumptions. I live in Suffolk, where thirteen people were executed in the happy republican days of the 1650s for the crime of being wandering gypsies. Outside Bury there is a site provided by the County Council under the 1968 Act and run by the Borough Council.

One gypsy, Richard Oakley, followed Sir George Young's advice and bought a nearby plot at the Paddocks, Rushbrooke Lane, where he grazes his horses, and installed his mobile home and touring caravan there. The Council's committee refused him planning permission to stay there, and, bearing in mind the government's change of policy, Mr Oakley appealed to the Secretary of State against the council decision. The Inspector dismissed his appeal as "he did not consider Mr Oakley's family background alone was a sufficiently special matter for him to disregard the emerging local plan" and added that his premises "were entirely inappropriate features in a Special Landscape Area". The inspector added that he did not share "the view that screening made the site unobtrusive" and argued that the "conifer hedge, trimmed in neat, suburban style, was totally out of place in the Suffolk countryside". You can cut down a conifer hedge in ten minutes, and I think it frivolous for the Inspector to make our shared disdain for the wrong kind of gardening an issue in what was bound to be a national test case. For there have been plenty of others.

But what about those other travelling people who aren't gypsies, and are generally called, rightly or wrongly, New Age Travellers. They and their families take to the road in old coaches. Their harassment by the police makes national news. They too encounter landowners who are happy to provide sites for them. This is not surprising at a time when landowners are being subsidised for taking land out of cultivation. Once again the obstacle is not private control of land-use, but the planning legislation. The most recent and much publicised of ventures of this kind is a site near the village of Norton Sub Hamden in Somerset. The residents there applied for planning permission for seven benders and tents to accommodate up to twelve adults on the 40-acre woodland site which includes a 1,000-tree apple orchard, some farm animals and organic allotments on the land that *they* own.

The District Council refused planning permission and issued an enforcement order, requiring them to remove themselves within six months. On 5th April 1995, the Inspector from the Department of the Environment held his public inquiry and concluded that the appellants were engaged in a unique experiment in low-impact living and small-scale agriculture and should be given the chance to show what could be done. He concluded that the experiment did not harm the Special Landscape Area in which it was situated, and added that although the residents were not gypsies in the normally accepted sense, the DoE Circular 1/94 advising local authorities to encourage gypsies to acquire land for their own residence, "does have some bearing on the case".

The Inspector, evidently fearing that his recommendation that the dwellers should be allowed to stay, urged that they should be given at least a year of security since their children were attending local schools from which they should not be hastily wrenched.

However, the Secretary of State overruled his Inspector and demanded that the settlers should be evicted within six months. The letter written on his behalf said that the aspirations of the residents were a:

> "personal preference which does not justify setting aside the planning objection. Any benefit of these aims to the rural economy would be negligible, since minimal agricultural and other produce would be available for wider consumption. And the reduction in demand for conventional housing and other claimed social benefits would be minimal. The view is taken that the provision of groups of tents or similar residential accommodation in the open countryside, merely to provide a

subsistence living for the occupants, is not a practical pattern of land use."

The residents of Tinker's Bubble are now trying to raise the £5,000 appeal fee in order to appeal against the Secretary of State's decision.

Now neither of these instances – that of the gypsy at Bury St Edmunds, nor the settlers at Tinker's Bubble – involve trespass, so the Criminal Justice and Public Order Act of 1994 is not applicable. The civil liberties body Liberty has issued a report called *Criminalising Diversity, Criminalising Dissent* analysing the first year of the operations of the Act for the new offences of 'aggravated trespass' and 'trespassory assembly'. It found that of the 346 cases of people arrested for aggravated trespass, more than half had the charges dropped and that the first CJA case against squatters collapsed in Bristol in October 1995. It also found that the *threat* of the Act was very widely used "in pursuit of a nationwide clampdown on diversity and dissent".

Meanwhile the number of people who have been rejected by the formal economy and the formal housing system, and who themselves reject the values of the official system, increases. As with the urban squatters' movement, there has to be some kind of accommodation, unless we are to see the affluent and powerful penalising the poor and powerless, for ever. Simon Fairlie, one of the settlers at Tinker's Bubble, put it succinctly when he observed that "it is the planning system, rather than ownership, that is now the main way in which ordinary people are prevented from 'reclaiming the land'."

Back in the 1960s a perceptive quartet of writers, Reyner Banham, Paul Barker, Peter Hall and Cedric Price published an article called 'Non-Plan: an experiment in freedom', urging that there should be Plan-Free zones, for people to do their own thing. They said that "at the least, one would find out what people want; at the most, one might discover the hidden style of mid-twentieth century Britain".

I took up the theme, drawing upon the experience of the pre-war 'plotlands' when I had the chance to address members of the New Town hierarchy in 1975. I urged that since the then still existing New Town Development Corporations controlled very large areas of land, one of them should sponsor an experiment in the relaxation of planning and building controls to make it possible for those who wanted to, to experiment in alternative ways of building and servicing houses, and in permitting a dwelling to be occupied in a most rudimentary condition for gradual completion. My paper argued that it should be possible to operate some kind of *usufruct*, some sort of leasehold with safeguards against purely cynical exploitation, which would enable people to house themselves in their own style and provide themselves with a means of livelihood, while not draining immense sums from central or local government.

The notion gained some support within Milton Keynes Development Corporation, from the chairman, Jock Campbell, down, and there were endless negotiations between a local body the Green Town Group, the Development Corporation and the Town and Country Planning Association. It all came to nothing because it was a matter of principle for the Development Corporation to avoid argument with the local planning authority, the County Council. As Don Ritson of the Development Corporation, remarked: "We can't get planning permission, even in outline, without a clear statement of what is to happen on the site, but if we specify what is to happen we are limiting in advance the aspirations of the people who we expect to settle there. And the whole idea is to give them the freedom of choice."

The concept was taken up at Telford New Town for a site that had been ravaged by old coal workings and unsuitable for ordinary development. At Lightmoor fourteen families, intended to be the first of four hundred, built their own homes and did their own thing. The terrible irony was that the activities of these original pioneers so upgraded the value of the intended extension that in the changed economic climate the site became considered too valuable for such a marginal settlement.

As in the case of the squatters of the 1960s, something has to yield. The Criminal Justice Act is too vindictive and punitive a law to become the determinant of who is entitled to live where. There has to be some kind of an accommodation between the ideology of Nimbyism – Not in My Back Yard – and the ordinary basic needs of the people excluded from the enterprise economy.

Over two hundred years ago, at the time of the Enclosures, Thomas Spence delivered a lecture at Newcastle-Upon-Tyne, with the enjoyable title, 'A Lecture Read at the Philosophical Society in Newcastle on November 8th 1775, for Printing of Which the Society

Did the Author the Honour to Expel Him'. Spence was arguing against the concept of *ownership* of land, since it was evident that the first landlords were "usurpers and tyrants; and all who have since possessed their lands, have done so by right of inheritance, purchase, etc., from them; and the present proprietors, like their predecessors, are proud to own it; and like them too, they exclude all others from the least pretence to their respective properties".

He concluded that:

> "...any one of them still can, by laws of their own making, oblige every living creature to remove off his property (which, to the great distress of mankind is too often put into execution); so of consequence were all the landowners to be of one mind, and determined to take their properties into their own hands, all the rest of mankind might go to heaven if they would, for there would be no place found for them here."

This is, of course, the precise intention of the Criminal Justice Act of 1994. Its conceivers, like the landed aristocracy of the eighteenth century, have a punitive world-view which excludes completely the unofficial history of housing that I have tried to explore in these seminars. And the planning system has become the unwitting accomplice of landlordism.

In the post-war decades popular mythology held that every acre of Britain was precious in the interests of agriculture. Farmers were free to destroy woodlands and hedges, drain wetlands and pollute rivers and water supplies in the interests of increased production. Now that the bubble of over-production has burst, the same people are subsidised for not growing and for returning habitats to what is seen as nature. This results in golf courses and publicly-financed set-aside.

Unofficial settlements are seen as a threat to wildlife, which is sacrosanct. The planning system is the vehicle that supports four-wheel-drive Range Rovers, but not the local economy, and certainly not those travellers and settlers seeking their own modest place in the sun. The system has to yield, unless we are prepared to see the 21st century as another period of persecution and suppression of understandable and natural human aspirations.

I would like you to explore the ways in which a place could be found for dissent and nonconformity, if only because the most interesting people we encounter are dissenters and nonconformists, in housing as in every other sphere of life. You will have noticed that the issue of legal access to land is not actually the key issue. In the gypsy instance, the case of Mr Oakley was not unique. Gypsy families at Lydia Park, near Guildford in Surrey bought their site twelve years ago, but even though the local council and Surrey county council accepted their colony of mobile homes, the Environment Secretary, John Gummer has intervened, once again, to determine whether or not they may stay there. And besides the case of Tinker's Bubble, there are other settlements which are completely legal in terms of tenure, where the new style of travelling people have been moved on by the planning machinery.

These people have bypassed the sacred rights of tenure, but still find their modest aspirations frustrated by the operations of planning legislation. Nobody actually planned such a situation. No professional planner would claim that his or her task was to grind unofficial housing out of existence, and nor would any of the local enforcers of the Building Regulations.

But all these unhappy confrontations are the direct result of public policy. Something has to be done to change it.

References and Sources

Angus Fraser (1992) *The Gypsies*, Blackwell.

Isabel Fonseca (1995) *Bury Me Standing: The Gypsies and their Journey*, Chatto.

Liberty (1995) *Criminalising Diversity, Criminalising Dissent: a report on the use of the public order provision in the Criminal Justice and Public Order Act 1994.*

Carey Newson (1995) 'Bubble Trouble', *Housing*, October, Vol. 31, No. 8.

Simon Fairlie (1995) 'The Problem With Planning', *Squall*, No. 11, Autumn (PO Box 8959, London, N19 5HW).

Reyner Banham, Paul Barker, Peter Hall & Cedric Price (1969) 'Non-Plan: An experiment in freedom', *New Society*, 20 March , Vol. 26, pp. 435-43.

Colin Ward (1975) 'The Do It Yourself New Town' (Garden Cities/New Towns Forum) printed in Colin Ward (1990) *Talking Houses*, Freedom Press.

Dennis Hardy (1991) *From New Towns to Green Politics*, E. and F.N. Spon.

Thomas Spence (1920) 'A Lecture Delivered at Newcastle 1775' in Max Beer (Ed.) *The Pioneers of Land Reform*, G. Bell & Sons.

Water and the gift relationship

I have been working on a book about the social and moral issues around water, seen both in a British context and globally. So I am grateful to Julian Le Grand because it was a chance conversation with him that led me to re-read Richard Titmuss's book about blood. I read it when it appeared in 1970 as *The Gift Relationship*, and I suppose that I was disappointed that it didn't have the breadth and range of his books on social policy. Wrongly, I dismissed it as an elaborate and specialised restatement of Kropotkin's *Mutual Aid*, filled with indigestible tables about the pale yellow fluid known as plasma and its constituents like immunoglobulin.

When Julian urged me to read it again, I found that my County Library had a copy in its reserve stock, stored, like plasma for my needs, and I changed my view. Titmuss died in 1974 and consequently did not live to see the full impact of the phenomenon that he called "the Philistine resurrection of economic man in social policy" but the event that sparked off his investigation was a publication from 1968 from the Institute of Economic Affairs called *The Price of Blood* making an economic case against a monopoly of altruism in blood transfusion. So he embarked on a comparison of the commercial market in bought blood with the voluntary donation of blood.

He found that the dominant characteristic of the American blood banking system was a redistribution of blood and blood products from the poor to the rich, since the sellers tended to be the unskilled, unemployed and other "low income groups and categories of exploited people". He found that when voluntary donors in Britain were asked about their motives "the vividness, individuality and diversity of their responses add life and a sense of community to the statistical generalities", but that 80% of answers suggested feelings of social responsibility towards other members of society.

Titmuss concluded that on four testable non-ethical criteria, the commercial trade in blood was bad:

"In terms of economic efficiency it is highly wasteful of
blood; shortages, chronic and acute, characterise the
demand and supply position and make illusory the
concept of equilibrium. It is administratively inefficient
and results in more bureaucratisation and much greater
administrative, accounting and computer overheads. In
terms of price per unit of blood to the patient (or
consumer) it is a system which is five to fifteen times
more costly than the voluntary system in Britain. And
finally, in terms of quality, commercial markets are much
more likely to distribute contaminated blood ..."

He allowed himself a flourish of rhetoric about his subject, when he
observed that:

"There is a bond that links all men and women in the
world so closely and intimately that every difference of
colour, religious belief and cultural heritage is
insignificant beside it ... composed of 55% water, the life
stream of blood that runs in the veins of very member of
the human race proves that the family of man is a reality.
Thousands of years ago man discovered that this fluid
was vital to him and precious beyond price."[1]

Blood, as the saying goes, is thicker than water. Blood is an individual
possession, water is a common necessity. But there are parallels
between the two, since water, that holds together the constituents of
blood, is equally vital for survival. As Michael Allaby explains, "a
person deprived of water will survive for no more than about six
days, or in a hot environment perhaps for as little as two or three".
   So water too, is in the words that Titmuss used, precious beyond
price. And somebody has to restate the self-evident fact that this
continually renewed but not inexhaustible resource belongs to
everybody. This is not to say that those who deliver it should not be
rewarded. The water-seller is part of an ancient service industry.
   The British are famous for grumbling about the weather, but are
blessed with an equable climate that most of the world would envy.
I live in rural East Anglia which has less than half the national
average rainfall. Our house, like those of the neighbours, was

connected to a piped water supply as recently as 1952. Until that year the most important items of water engineering for the occupants were the well and a collection of galvanised iron buckets, filled every day from the well for drinking and cooking, from tanks draining the roof gutters for washing, and from the pond fed by field drains for watering the garden and the animals. Water was never wasted because every member of every family, apart from those who employed servants, knew the incessant labour of carrying it.

The deeper the well, the purer the water, but the greater the labour. It is not surprising that as the technology improved, the village pump became a focus of rural life. We use the expression 'parish pump politics' as a derisory way of describing small local issues, but the pump is a powerful symbol of community effort.

Indeed, Brian Bailey, the historian, not of parish pumps but of village greens, suggests that:

> "One possibility which has not been proposed, as far as I know, is that small greens were conceived as central areas reserved for the protection of the common water supply and to give access to it. It is easy for us in these days of piped water to every home to overlook how the absolutely overriding consideration in the establishment of any village or hamlet was the availability of water. When a well was dug, with great labour, to supply all the villagers with their water, it must have been regarded with a protective reverence that we find hard to imagine today."[2]

He gives a topographical account of a long series of parish pumps and the inscriptions on them and remarks how, though now obsolete, they are "often carefully protected from vandals and pollution. They stand like symbols of village continuity and the community's source of life".

But since he wrote attitudes have changed. At Blockley in Gloucestershire, there is an arch protecting a spout from a natural spring, and incised in the pediment above is the legend 'Water from the Living Rock: God's Precious Gift to Man'. It is called the Russell Spring, from the family that connected it for public use 150 years ago "at a time when cholera was rife in the area". In 1994 a newly formed Cotswold Water Company applied to the National Rivers

Authority for an abstraction licence to bottle and sell 750 gallons a day. The anecdote is a parable of the coarsening of British sensitivity to the nature of a universal human need.

There is, of course, a direct relationship between the size of a human settlement and the need for safe water and safe sewage disposal, but the mushroom growth of British towns and cities coincided with the spread of the ideology that the market and private enterprise would solve all human problems, while public enterprise was wasteful and wicked. Private water companies supplied that minority of households that could afford a piped water supply, people were prosecuted for the crime of stealing water, but the affluent as well as the poor added to the appalling death rate from diseases like dysentery, typhoid fever and cholera. In Liverpool in 1844 Samuel Holme was arguing that:

> "... water is as essential to the health and comfort of mankind as the air we breathe, and when mankind congregate in masses counted only by tens of thousands, it is essential to the public health that it should be most abundant, not doled out to yield 30% interest, but supplied from the public rates and at net cost."[3]

His view triumphed and was enshrined by a clause in the Public Health Acts which declared that a house without an adequate supply was 'unfit for human habitation'. Most private suppliers were bought by local authorities, supplying every household. Some remained as 'statutory undertakers' governed by the same rules and with a limitation on dividends. Bill Luckin, the historian of the River Thames, remarks on the change in official attitudes among technical, scientific and medical investigators, that:

> "To them, at least, whatever may have been their doubts about the explicitly political implications of municipalism, interventionism and collectivism, 'the salvation of the city' was nothing less than a binding moral duty."[4]

The post-war Labour government, which took gas and electricity out of the control of local authorities, left water alone. It was a Conservative government which brought, in the Water Act of 1973, what was thought to bring a coherent approach to water supply, river management and sewage disposal.

As Fred Pearce put it in his study of Britain's water crisis:

> "In 1974 the new broom of local government re-organisation swept away 100 water boards, fifty local council water undertakings, seven water committees, 27 river authorities, two river conservancies, 1,366 council sewerage undertakings and 27 joint sewerage authorities and replaced them with ten regional water authorities to cover the whole of England and Wales. The new authorities had power over the whole 'water cycle' from upland reservoirs to seagoing sludge ships; from land drainage to water mains and from pollution control to flood prevention. The only survivors from the old system were thirty water companies, which were saved by Conservative ministers. The new authorities are strange hybrid bodies, neither nationalised industry, nor local government ... And behind them all is a National Water council appointed by ministers ..."[5]

This regime was swept away by the government's sale of the water industry in November 1989, which according to some estimates "left the Government £1.4 billion out of pocket on the deal". Other estimates think the loss was greater. This grotesque venture illustrates the willingness of government to listen to people taking extreme cases as intellectual exercises. Titmuss felt obliged to respond in detail to the test case of *The Price of Blood*, an insignificant item in the market economy, but enormously significant in the moral economy. He provided a detailed refutation on one particular issue, and someone will do the same for water, which is far more complicated since it involves a whole series of topics.

The first is that households in Britain are having their water supply cut off because of non-payment of water bills.

Where I live, tenants of local authorities paid a small sum in their weekly rent for water, once controlled by the same council. Today the council declines to be a collecting agency for a private company and the vastly increased water bill, payable in advance, has become another of the overhead costs of living which poor people have, somehow, to budget for. Until 1988 people in receipt of the government's 'supplementary benefit' had their water bills paid, but with the abolition of that payment, they too became responsible for finding the money. Privatisation of water supply brought a new aggressively commercial approach to the poorest of water users. Thousands had their water supply cut off, an act that I had imagined to be illegal, as it is in Scotland and Northern Ireland. I was wrong, and the representative of Thames Water told the press in 1992 that "we are being too soft, and that is why our disconnection level will rise".[6] A handful of members of parliament, led by Helen Jackson, have sought to introduce legislation to require the water companies to recover outstanding payments through the courts, like any other creditor, and not by disconnection.[7] They have not succeeded, despite their accumulation of countless case-histories of disadvantaged people penalised by the ruthless policies of water companies.

At a meeting Helen Jackson convened in 1993, John Middleton, director of public health for the Sandwell Health Authority in the West Midlands, drew attention to the collapse of a sense of public morality since the sanitary campaigns of 150 years ago, recalling that "the Victorians at least recognised the need to provide safe, wholesome water supplies for everybody, rich and poor. Water disconnection is something we should not tolerate in a civilised society." He said that during the period of 1991 and 1992, with a marked rise in disconnection in his area in which over 1,400 households lost their water supply, "over this period cases of hepatitis and dysentery rose tenfold".[8] When the British Medical Association examined the same issue it found that there were a number of vulnerable groups for whom a guaranteed water supply was vital.[9] They were people with medical conditions requiring the use of additional water for bathing or washing clothing, young children and elderly people. When the Policy Studies Institute initiated a careful study of water debt and disconnection it found that "of these, only elderly customers seemed to have a low risk of water debt and hence of disconnection". It also reported that "during 1994 about two million households fell into arrears with their water bills and 12,500 ended up disconnected from the water supply".[10]

The second vital issue concerns the water industry's attitudes and public attitudes to water shortage.

The British Isles are water-rich, with adequate rainfall, but occasionally experience a water shortage. It is fascinating to compare public attitudes to drought conditions in 1995 with those that emerged in the sixteen dry months between May 1975 and August 1976. British households in 1976 were unaware of future shifts in perception that changed water from a common good to a commercial product. Fred Pearce, trying to interpret the lessons of the drought, reported how until then water planners had seen "any form of supply restriction – even an hosepipe ban – as an admission of their failure. They realised that it was nonsense to spend millions to cut the frequency of hosepipe bans from one year in five to one year in ten". Yet he also learned about the improvisations of the then regional water authorities in pooling access to water sources, as well as their long-term plans like the London ring main and the device of recharging aquifers from winter river water.

The public response was even more interesting. The National Water Council found that:

> "the potential for voluntary savings by the public and industry during a water crisis was vast. The 'save it' publicity campaign during the drought cut water demand by 30% in some areas ... and further measures like emergency leak detection and pressure reductions in the mains made savings of another 10%."[11]

Ninety percent of the population answered pleas to cut down on bathwater, and over eighty percent said that they had taken more care to put the plug in basins and sinks, though only nine percent said that they had put a brick in the WC cistern. In 1976 there was intense co-operation between water authorities, so that Fred Pearce notes that "in the worst drought for 250 years, engineers managed to keep water flowing". There was active co-operation from the public in reducing demand. There were no recriminations; simply a willingness to learn from the experience.

By the time of the drought of 1995, the climate had changed. The public placed the blame on the water companies and the companies blamed the public. The Secretary of State for the Environment, John Gummer, advised people to follow the precepts of 1976 and recycle washing-up water on the garden and put a brick in the WC cistern.

My local newspaper, which is hardly a radical journal, pointed in a leading article to the crucial difference between then and now:

> "But then water was public property, and the public had an interest in conserving it. We have since been re-educated by Mr Gummer and his Cabinet colleagues, to think of water not as a natural resource, but as a capitalist product.
>
> Newly-privatised water companies have sought to justify exorbitant profits by telling us what a vastly improved service they are providing. They have rewarded themselves with enormous 'performance-related' pay rises. Are we not entitled to expect that, as long as we pay our bills, we should be able to use just as much of the stuff as we like? And should it matter to the profit-centred water companies whether we choose to use it for watering our gardens or flushing the loo? Isn't the buyer entitled to use it as he likes – just like any other commercial product?
>
> Of course, such attitudes do not fit well with conservation, but if conservation had been properly considered at the time, perhaps privatisation would not have seemed such a good idea."[12]

The theme of conservation, so very much dependent on public attitudes, raises another, vital, water issue. International bodies and home-grown advisers like the Royal Commission on Environmental Pollution have advised on the quality of water, the discharge of effluents into rivers and seas and, as anyone who goes to the seaside knows, have found the British system wanting. We have inherited the water infrastructure of the nineteenth century and have failed to adapt it to the 21st century standards. This provides endless difficulties. Is it sensible to use water purified to exacting standards for washing the car or for irrigating potatoes? Explaining their unwillingness to meet water and sewage purification standards, the present government blames the lack of capital investment in the past, and we continually hear that the rise in water charges since privatisation is explained by the need for new capital investment that hasn't actually happened.

The fact, of course, is that the changes of 1974 brought the supply of water for the first time under direct Treasury control, and that under both Conservative and Labour governments, the spending of water authorities was steadily reduced between 1974 and 1986. By 1982 the government was permitting the water industry to spend only half the sum it put into capital investment in 1974.

Here is an issue which ought to involve anyone considering water supply in the context of social policy and public administration. In the period when water supply and sewage disposal were found to be a binding moral duty, not a matter of ability to pay, inland towns and cities, like, say, Birmingham, embarked on vast, far-ranging water supply engineering, bringing water from the Welsh mountains to cope with need, as well as building sewage farms discharging a clean final flow. Coastal towns, before the holiday boom and the shift to a large permanent population, discharged raw sewage into the sea, neglecting to construct treatment plants. In the transfer to direct government control, just as the consequences of pollution from government-subsidised nitrate fertilisers, herbicides and pesticides to water sources became evident, direct Treasury control of spending, cut back on water and drainage investment. In the new era of privatisation, our relations with the water industry are conducted through the medium of public relations, and the citizen has to rely on pressure groups to learn what is going on.

Calls for responsible behaviour from resentful water users are met with a derisive response. This is a direct result of redefining water as a commodity. Last month the Secretary of State for the Environment revealed the British government's plans to create a free market in water.

For the DoE, John Gummer, announced that he proposed to allow, first companies using an annual 250 megalitres to buy water from a supplier other than their local company, and to extend this eventually to every consumer. He explained that "competition is the best guarantee for consumers that they receive value for money, better services and lower prices". He said nothing about the desirability of limiting the demand for water. Speaking for the parliamentary opposition, Frank Dobson commented that "these proposals do nothing about the fundamental failings of the privatised water industry with its soaring prices, profits and bosses' pay and perks. It does nothing to stop the scandal of the environmental damage of taking too much water from rivers and lakes during dry spells".[13]

His party, however, has announced no plans for the de-privatisation of the water supply industry if and when it takes office, nor which of the previous regimes it would favour. Least of all has it asked how we could all be involved. There is indeed a void in organisational thinking in the field of community control of local services. The alternatives are perceived as public bureaucracy or private profit.

A week before the British parliament debated the proposal to introduce competition in the water industry, the municipal council of the town of Grenoble in south-east France was considering a proposal to return it to municipal control. France, like Britain experienced a vogue for marketising public services in the 1980s, with two huge companies, Compagnie Generale des Eaux and Lyonnaise des Eaux as the beneficiaries. Grenoble's municipal water undertaking was sold to the latter company in 1989 and the experience of citizens has been much like that of British equivalents, with the additional factor that it was reported in 1994 that "Lyonnaise subsidiaries in Grenoble and Lyon are suspected by local judges of funnelling funds to conservative parties in exchange for contract favours. No illegality has yet been proved".[14] However, there was widespread public outrage, as in Britain, at the results of privatisation, and a coalition of opposition councillors called *Démocratie/Ecologie/Solidarité* tabled a motion demanding a return to public control of water. They were outflanked when the Mayor announced a deal for a mixed water economy with the Town owning 51% and Lyonnaise des Eaux 49%, accompanied by a retrospective reduction of water bills from 1st January 1996. The coalition split apart over this deal, which some of them claimed as a victory, while others saw it as a defeat.[15]

The British have been led to believe that France was the most centralised country in Europe, a dubious honour that should undoubtedly be awarded to the United Kingdom. It is impossible to conceive any British city regaining a controlling interest in its own water supply in the current political climate. But the devastating conclusion we are bound to draw from the insular debate is that a crisis of social responsibility has been reduced to a matter of buying in the cheapest market.

In practice, of course, the domestic consumer will never have a choice of supplier in Britain, and considering the cost in energy resources of pumping water around the country, the idea is unsound, especially in ecological terms.

But there is also in fact a conflict between the lobby for water as a common good, and the Green or conservationist lobby, when it suggests the use of the price mechanism as the means of discouraging us from wasting it.

In 1887 the anarchist propagandist Peter Kropotkin saw "water supplied to private dwellings, with a growing tendency towards disregarding the exact amount of it used by the individual" as one of the signs, along with free roads, free libraries, free public schools, parks and paved and lighted streets for everyone's use, as part of a trend towards a society where "everybody, contributing for the common well-being to the full extent of his capacities, shall enjoy also from the common stock of society to the fullest possible extent of his needs".[16]

A century later acceptable opinion had made huge shifts, for two reasons. The first was the rise of the revived religion of the market and in the privatisation of public goods at any cost. The second was the growth of ecological consciousness and the realisation that all resources are finite. For example, Sandra Postel, a renowned authority on water scarcity remarks that: "Amazingly, water charges for most British households are linked to the value to their home, and have nothing to do with actual consumption ... Trials in the United Kingdom have shown that metering can cut household use there by 10-15%".[17]

The Organisation for Economic Co-operation and Development (OECD) is an intergovernmental body of 24 industrialised countries. In the 1980s it formed a steering group to advise on economic aspects of water conservation, since "for both economic and environmental reasons it has become increasingly difficult to meet water demands in their various forms". It found a great variety of pricing structures for water provision, and classified them into five types of payment for piped services in water supply, sewerage and sewage treatment.[18]

1. *Flat rate tariffs* where water charges are not directly related to quantities of water used (this is the method commended by Kropotkin and condemned by Sandra Postel, above). At the beginning of 1996, 93% of the British population still had an unmeasured supply, but the government, and the Director of the

regulatory body Ofwat argue that a measured supply is the best long-term solution to water shortages, cutting consumption by 11%. A report from the Centre for the Study of Regulated Industries showed that the average water charges for people with meters had fallen by nearly 2% in England, while unmetered consumers had witnessed a rise of 39% in water charges. The opposition spokesman, Frank Dobson claimed that "the government had a secret agenda to force everybody to install meters".[19]

2. *Average cost pricing* where all water service costs, other than access costs, are grouped together and divided among the total number of units expected to be sold, to generate a unit cost. The OECD investigators did not investigate the degree to which private profit-making water suppliers, might enhance the average costs for the benefit of shareholders or directors, nor to finance speculative investment outside the water industry. This has been the subsequent experience of the sale of the water industry to private monopolies in England and Wales.

3. *Declining block tariffs* where succeeding blocks of units of water consumed are sold at lower and lower prices. A fixed or minimum billing charge is usually included.

4. *Increasing or progressive block tariffs* where succeeding blocks or units of water are sold at higher and higher prices. The OECD report found that "these tariffs were becoming increasingly common, and reflected, at least initially, income redistribution objectives (provision of an initial, basic supply at a low rate, with additional consumption becoming progressively more expensive)." The OECD reported too, that "the system was used to promote efficiency and conservation objectives, although it is noted that the evidence of the effectiveness of such tariffs in the industrial sector is not clear, given the concurrent economic recession and restructuring away from large water using industries". This is a bland way of reporting that industrial use of water has declined in the industrialised nations through the collapse of heavy industry.

5. *Two-part tariffs* including a fixed element, often varying according to some characteristic of the user, and average cost pricing in the

form of a single volumetric charge. These too, might be seen as a recognition of a universal right to water: a basic notional fee for the right of access and a subsequent fee for the quantity used, above a minimum.

The OECD report also noted a wide variation in the concept of 'natural' water services, and vast variations in the attitude to irrigation water. The demand for water for irrigation was "highly responsive to price changes". Its conclusions were that in order to ensure the most efficient use of a scarce natural resource, the principle of 'marginal cost pricing' should be adopted. The idea that water is a common good became marginal. The investigators found the concept of equity or fairness as "a difficult objective to define" since it ranged from the notion of social pricing, "whereby no consumer should be prevented by income considerations from enjoying the benefits of water, to narrower concepts such as that provided by the requirement that each consumer should pay the same per unit of water service received regardless of its cost". Inevitably, across 24 nation states, it found that:

> "In some countries, water pricing is structured to foster development in agricultural and industrial sectors, to lighten charges on isolated communities or to help low-income households; in others the view is taken that it is preferable to adopt an economically efficient water pricing system in combination with a social security system for those consumers disadvantaged by the policy. It was thought that any financial subsidies to the water services as a whole, or to one group or water service users from another, should be made explicit and be justified by arguments for special treatment."[20]

The hasty sale of the water supply industry in England and Wales ignored the need for any special treatment. And you will know that social security help is no longer available for the payment of water charges. You will also know that increasingly the water companies are adopting a system of 'smart cards' or keys rechargeable at the post office for prepayment for domestic water. The supply is charged for, not on the basis of quantity but of time. If credit runs out and another payment is not made, the supply is cut off automatically after seven days. The legality of this system is to be tested in the courts.

In the nineteenth century, people learned the hard way that water *must* be seen as a common good. The current Philistine resurrection, as Titmuss foresaw, of economic man in social policy, is not only a betrayal of the poor, but is also an obstacle in the way of working out an ecologically sound and responsible approach to water supply and disposal in the next century. The tragedy is that none of us knows the road back to the ancient wisdom that as a need as vital as blood, water has to be both shared and conserved.

Notes and References

1. Richard M. Titmuss (1970) *The Gift Relationship: From Human Blood to Social Policy*, London: Allen & Unwin.

2. Brian Bailey (1985) *The English Village Green*, London: Robert Hale.

3. Derek Fraser (1979) *Power and Authority in the Victorian City*, Oxford: Blackwell.

4. Bill Luckin (1986) *Pollution and Control: A Social History of the Thames in the Nineteenth Century*, London: Adam Hilger.

5. Fred Pearce (1982) *Watershed: The Water Crisis in Britain*, London: Junction Books.

6. *The Guardian*, 2 September 1992.

7. *Hansard* (House of Commons Report) 25 Nov. 1992, 28 Jan. 1993, 25 Feb. 1993.

8. *The Independent*, 29 January 1993.

9. British Medical Association (1994) *Water: A Vital Resource*, London: BMA.

10. Alicia Herbert and Elaine Kempson (1995) *Water Debt and Disconnection*, London: Policy Studies Institute.

11. National Water Council (1976) *The 1975-6 Drought*, London.

12. Leading article in *The East Anglian Daily Times*, 22 August 1995.

13. *Hansard* (House of Commons Report), 1 April 1996.

14. *The Guardian*, 9 November 1994.

15. 'L'eau devise la majorité', *Le Dauphiné* (Grenoble) 26 March 1996.

16. Peter Kropotkin (1887) *Anarchist Communism: Its Basis and Principles*, (London: Freedom Press, 1987).

17. Sandra Postel (1992) *The Last Oasis: Facing Water Scarcity*, London: Worldwatch/Earthscan.

18. Paul Herrington (1987) *Pricing of Water Services*, Paris: OECD.

19. 'Water meters, secret agenda', *The Guardian*, 21 February 1996.

20. Herrington, *op. cit.*

Anarchism in the 21st century

I must begin by congratulating the London School of Economics on its centenary, but I need to add a second, grateful word of praise to the School as an institution, in inviting a marginal person like me as a visitor. This has given me a great deal of pleasure, most especially because of the stimulating encounters I have had this year in this academic rabbit-warren.

You will know better than me that any institution like yours gets associated with the opinions of vocal professors, so that a teaching and learning body has, in the outside world, been seen, not as an academy of free enquiry but as a megaphone for the views of particular teachers. Even in my own lifetime I have learned that the LSE was the mouthpiece of Fabian managerial centralism, or of automatic robot Marxism, or alternatively, of propaganda for unrestricted free market capitalism.

Naturally I'm aware that all these views are caricatures, associating particular teachers with the institution that employs them, but of course I am bound to ask what has become of the centralising, bureaucratic Fabianism of the Webbs, or of Laski's Marxism, or of von Hayek's road to serfdom, when it is obvious to all of us that the aim of the flexible labour market of today's economy is to reduce us all to the all-too-real serfdom of child labour in the poorest corners of global exploitation?

We have inherited the Christian calendar and one historical trend it brings with it is the tendency for outbursts of revivalism towards the end of the centuries, especially noted at the end of millennia and semi-millennia. I make this generalisation from the period leading up to the year 1000 and the year 1500. We have another of these accidental turning-points coming up, and, since we live in a secular age in the West at least, the revival has been expressed in commercial rather than spiritual terms.

I am talking about the religion of market values which has swept across with the fervour of the Protestant Reformation, or of Method-ism at the end of the eighteenth century, or evangelical revivalism at the end of the nineteenth century.

Everyone here will be aware that it has even changed our language and hence the way we think about goods and services. There is something rather sinister and frightening about the sheer speed with which in so many fields in which relationships based on an ideology of reciprocity and mutual obligation have been replaced by real or simulated market values. Now you and I, having watched the ebb and flow of many a fashion, know that the evangelical phase of the current worship of the market isn't going to last, for the same reasons that impelled the early nineteenth century sanitary reformers to report on the horrors of the old sanctification of the market, or Engels to write his book on the *Condition of the Working Class in England*. People will have to invent alternatives in the 21st century, just as they were obliged to in the nineteenth.

One of these alternatives is undoubtedly going to be anarchism. The word, as you know, means 'contrary to authority' or 'without government', and for a definition of the political ideology I always turn to the article written by Peter Kropotkin for the eleventh edition of the *Encyclopaedia Britannica*. He defined anarchism as:

> "The name given to a principle or theory of life and conduct under which society is conceived without government – harmony in such a society being obtained, not by submission to law, or by obedience to any authority, but by free agreements concluded between the various groups, territorial and professional, freely constituted for the sake of production and consumption, as also for the satisfaction of the infinite variety of needs and aspirations of a civilised being."[1]

I'm happy with that kind of definition, since he adds his endorsement of the federal principle, explaining that this mode of social organisation in which local bodies would "substitute themselves for the State" would represent "an interwoven network, composed of an infinite variety of groups and federations of all sizes and degrees, local, regional, national and international – temporary or more or less permanent – for all possible purposes: production, consumption and exchange, communications, sanitary arrangements, education, mutual protection, defence of the territory, and so on ..."

I also note that he was not describing some ideal society where history has somehow come to an end, since he adds that:

> "Moreover, such a society would represent nothing immutable. On the contrary – as is seen in organic life at large – harmony would (it is contended) result from an ever-changing adjustment and readjustment of equilibrium between the multitudes of forces and influences, and this adjustment would be the easier to obtain as none of the forces would enjoy a special protection from the State."

This is a polite way of asking what would happen to multinational capitalism if it could not rely on the armed forces of nation states to uphold its property rights in both rich and poor nations? Suppose that primary producers decided that it was more sensible to feed and clothe themselves, rather than make other people rich in grabbing an increasingly competitive slice of a global market?

Just as history hasn't happened in the way that Fabian or Marxist philosophers anticipated, so it has also failed to fulfil the hopes of the best-known anarchist thinkers. William Godwin, the rationalist, would have been surprised and appalled by the re- emergence of religious and nationalist fundamentalism. But so are all of us.

Pierre-Joseph Proudhon, the advocate of mutualism, would be appalled at the way the building societies, which began as organs of working-class self-help, have been tumbling over themselves to become capitalist banks. Indeed, I have argued myself in this building that British social policy took the wrong turning when the Fabians denigrated the whole edifice of self-help and mutual aid bodies built up since the early nineteenth century in favour of universal social welfare through the machinery of state. We have learned how vulnerable this is. Michael Bakunin, the apostle of insurrectionism, would have his rhetoric undermined by the fate of all popular insurrections since his day, but for the fact that in his disputes with Marx in the 1870s, he accurately forecasts the history of the Soviet Empire, with his well-known claim that while "liberty without socialism is privilege and injustice; socialism without liberty is slavery and brutality".[2]

Peter Kropotkin, the scientific optimist, would feel chastened by real events in the real world, but for several interesting utterances of

his late years. In 1919, in the midst of the civil war that followed the
Russian Revolution, he wrote that:

> "Today, after the cruel lessons of the last war, it should
> be clear to every serious person and above all to every
> worker, that such wars are inevitable so long as certain
> countries consider themselves destined to enrich
> themselves by the production of finished goods and
> divide the backward countries up among themselves, so
> that these countries provide the raw materials while they
> accumulate wealth themselves on the basis of the labour
> of others."

He was describing the consumer sovereignty that we experience
every week in the global supermarket, and in the same period, for
the post-war reprint of his book about work, *Fields, Factories and
Workshops*, he added a significant comment, that links him with
today's Green movement and its recognition of the folly of
assumptions of endless economic growth. For he explained that "it
pleads for a new economy in the energies used in supplying the
needs of human life, since these needs are increasing and the
energies are not inexhaustible".[3]

I think that there is a great deal to be learned from the anarchist
tradition, but I know that all ideological positions are hampered by
their past; hence the current dilemmas of all three major political
parties. A Dutch friend of mine, Rudolf de Jong, remarked recently
that if some selective virus killed off all the world's anarchists
tomorrow, as well as their ample literature, anarchism as an idea
would re-emerge in every kind of society.

So in looking for the re-emergence of anarchism in the 21st
century, I will forget the anarchist past and take as my guide a half-
remembered book by a veteran of social investigation and social
invention, known to everyone here, Michael Young. In 1958 he gave
a new word to the language in his satire *The Rise of the Meritocracy*,
allegedly the work of a future scholar whose conclusions are never
reached as his manuscript broke off during some 21st century
insurrection. This imaginary historian looks back on our own day as
one where "two contradictory principles for legitimising power were
struggling for mastery – the principle of kinship and the principle of

merit". Merit wins in the end with earlier and earlier educational selection, and a new non-self-perpetuating elite is formed of "the five per cent of the population who know what five per cent means". The top jobs go the top brains, and Payment by Merit (summarised in the formula M equals IQ plus Effort) widens the gap between top and bottom people. The people at the bottom are not only treated as inferior, they *know* that they are inferior.

New social tensions arise and a Populist movement arises, consisting of an alliance of rejected people with dissident intellectuals, mainly women. They produce the Chelsea Manifesto of the year 2009 which turns out to be the spark that eventually leads to the disturbances of 2033 and the gutting of the Department of Education. We don't know what happens next because the alleged historian loses his life in the Peterloo demonstration of 2034. You may remember that the Chelsea Manifesto declared that:

> "The classless society would be one which both possessed and acted upon plural values. Were we to evaluate people, not according to their intelligence and their education, their occupation and their power, but according to their kindliness and their courage, their imagination and sensibility, their sympathy and generosity, there could be no classes ... The classless society would also be the tolerant society, in which individual differences were actively encouraged as well as passively tolerated, in which full meaning was at last given to the dignity of man ..."[4]

Now of course Michael Young was writing his fantasy almost forty years ago in the far-off era of full employment. If he was producing it today, no doubt the letter E in his formula M equals IQ plus E would be changed from effort to Entrepreneurial Flair. But the preconditions for explosive resentment are with us today to a far greater extent that they were when he was writing. Just consider the implications of Will Hutton's lecture on 'The 30/30/40 society' printed in the March issue of the *RSA Journal*. He reminded us of the grisly new categorisation of British society, and he makes the implications clear:

"There is a bottom 30% of unemployed and economically
inactive who are marginalised; another 30% who, while
in work, are in forms of employment that are structurally
insecure; and there are only 40% who can count themselves as holding tenured jobs which allow them to regard
their income prospects with any certainty. But even the
secure top 40% know they are at risk; their numbers have
been shrinking steadily for twenty years."[5]

He goes on to describe the dilemmas and crises faced by each of
these groups. There is the fear for the bottom 30% that "marginalisation will change into complete social and economic exclusion" while
for the 30% of newly insecure "the social institutions and systems
built up over the past fifty years to protect against risk are decaying".
Meanwhile "the struggle to maintain living standards has meant ever
longer working hours" so that not only parenting suffers, but "the
capacity to sustain friendships outside work, to become a member of
local clubs and societies, to play a part in the local neighbourhood
reduces as hours worked rise".

Hutton concluded that "one day the pendulum will swing back
because it must." It certainly must. Hutton was retailing social facts
known to everyone here, and in considering the re-invention of
anarchism in the next century, I would like to take the last of his
points first. I am much influenced by a perception of a non-
anarchist, Martin Buber, in his lecture on 'Society and the State',
where distinguishing between the *social* principle and the *political*
principle he argued that the result of the dominance of the political
principle, of power, hierarchy and dominion over the social principle
of voluntary association for common need is "a continual diminution
of social spontaneity" in the form of the ability and willingness to
play a part in the community.[6]

This point of view had a very striking confirmation from another
non-anarchist source in a recent study of civic traditions in
modern Italy, *Making Democracy Work*, by Robert Putnam of
Harvard, Robert Leonardi of this School, and Raffaella Nanetti
from Chicago. This book has very recently been published in
translation in Italy, a country with a corrupt state apparatus but
a strong society in the North and a fatally weak social tradition in the
South.[7]

But let me turn to Hutton's main point, the fear that for a significant proportion of the population, "marginalisation will change into complete social and economic exclusion".

We are familiar with this phenomenon in American cities and it is now visible in European public housing estates. Research based in the School has shown how in Britain, 70% of tenants in the forlorn enclaves of public housing on the fringe of British cities are, for lack of work, obliged to depend on minimum benefits from the state and are consequently seen as a drag on the economy, rather than as a wasted human resource. Anne Power and her colleagues have reported on efforts to divert the government's window-dressing policies into attempts to support, rather than ignore, local self-organisation. One of her reports is called *Swimming Against the Tide*, and she reminds us that there are examples "of residents in very marginal areas taking over major responsibility for their areas in very difficult conditions and bringing about remarkable improvements through local organisation. This process enriches individual lives and transforms collective conditions".[8]

They are indeed swimming against the tide, and Dr Power reminds us that conflict on the estate in the 1990s is often *within* communities "between young tearaways and community activists". This is the time of year when people in housing management look at the weather and say that the joy-riding season has begun. She notes that the behaviour of young males, including their threatening and victimisation of objectors:

> "seemed to reflect deep alienation – indeed, several young joy-riders were killed in frantic getaway attempts. The police seemed powerless and, unlike in the 1980s, community leaders denounced their own young men, as well as the outside world. The actions of the youth were an attempt at short-term power against long-term hopelessness."[9]

Politicians of all parties respond with a series of punitive answers, like putting those of the wild young males into military corrective establishments or putting up for adoption the babies of the unsupported young females. Many of them revolve around the habit of blaming the underclass for its own fate, although the political añalyst Peter Kellner was bold enough to say: "My target is different. I blame the overclass".[10]

So do I. But I can recognise that the glib espousal of the supremacy of the market has consequences in the 21st century Predictions of the immediate future are determined more by temperament than by calculation of risks and likelihoods, and usually turn out to be wrong. It is usual to predict that the future will be like the present, only more so. We can look to North and South America and see the affluent barricaded in a private world run by private armies of security guards, while the ghettos of the poor are dominated by local thugs and drug barons with their terrifying juvenile acolytes.

Or we can study the long history of the concept of an underclass, and notice that it evaporates in periods of full employment. Its historian, John Macnicol, pointed out to me that the underclass was decimated by the fact that there were jobs for all both in Britain and the United States, and of course, in Germany, during the two world wars. Fortunately, the prospect of a Third World War is diminishing, unless we see it as a coming struggle between the global underclass of the poor world and the global masters of the rich nations, over resources which the poor lack and the rich squander.

My picture of the future has close links with the one that Michael Young described in his old satire, envisaging the Chelsea Manifesto of 2009 and the Peterloo demonstration of 2034. The Manifesto addresses the question of human dignity. Now what does the young urban criminal say in court or to the media when asked to explain his behaviour? He says words like, 'All I wanted was a bit of respect' or 'I hit him as he didn't show me any respect'. Human beings desperately want to be *valued*. Whether or not we deserve respect from fellow-citizens, we all care about human dignity, especially our own.

This is why, if I'm asked about anarchism in the 21st century, I see it emerging from endless local struggles for influence down on the estate. On one side are those heroines and heroes of local community action, battling for consensus over physical improvements, starting mother-and-baby groups, play-groups, food co-ops, credit unions, LETS ventures, and a whole range of activities built around communality and mutual aid and self-help. They are usually women with a load of family obligations of their own, and they teach themselves the complexities of coping with local government and the welfare system. On the other side are the vandals, arsonists, racists, joy-riders and drug-peddlers, quite apart from loan-sharks and tally-men exploiting the day-to-day, hand-to-mouth improvisatory economy of the poor.

The huge task is that of winning over the piratical Thatcherite individualists of the anti-social power of the young into the camp of social action and effective community power.

This approach has had few victories, though one of them was undoubtedly that of making the Poll Tax uncollectable.

You will recognise that I am talking about *social control*. This very equivocal phrase has two opposite meanings. It is usually taken to imply the way in which the rulers of a nation state manipulate the behaviour of citizens, through the police, the army if necessary, the legal and penal system, the management of information and the media. But the sociologist who coined the term 95 years ago, Edward Allsworth Ross, meant something quite different. He studied 'frontier' societies in nineteenth century America, a topic with which we are familiar from our lifetimes of watching Westerns. We know all about the goodies and baddies gradually enforcing the rule of law. Ross showed how social control was not achieved by romantic individualists, nor by the agents of remote government, but by the people who are bit players in the Western sagas: the women home-makers with a vested interest in continuity and security, the teacher (invariably a woman) in the little red schoolhouse, the newspaper editor and printer (invariably a man, wearing a green eye-shield) with his fearless publication of the truth, and the preacher reminding the powerful that if they gained the whole world they lost their own souls.[11]

It's a bit like that in today's forlorn estates, where nobody goes unless they live there or have business to transact there. They are our unglamorous internal frontiers on the underside of British society (and most of Europe has the same phenomenon). There is the same struggle to win support for social values against the rugged individualists and tough guys.

There is nothing surprising about the fact that another of your visiting professors, Stanley Cohen, in his pessimistic and honest book of ten years ago, discussing the work of crime and punishment, *Visions of Social Control*, concluded that "mutual aid, fraternity and good-neighbourliness still sound better than dependence on bureaucracies and professions" and that "this means coming back to the political philosophy most consistent with sociology, namely anarchism".[12]

Naturally I agree with him, but those of us who hold to this belief have a new burden to carry: that of the concept of 'communitarianism' favoured by Amitai Etzioni, welcomed among politicians of all parties both here and in the United States, where it turns out to be part of the culture of contentment, seeking to reduce the expense of welfare payments and of policing in the poverty belt that surrounds every American city. To me, community control, if and when it becomes effective, will result in devastating challenges for not only government but the controllers of capital and finance.

For we all know that the aim of the managers of capital today is to do without labour, and when it has to be hired, to do so on terms which are casual, part-time, and carry no obligations at all. The unemployed are blamed for not having the new computer skills that are in demand, but if they acquire them they find that e-mail and satellite communications enable tonight's software problem to be solved in Bangalore, India, with the answer beamed in tomorrow morning, by highly skilled workers earning a fraction of the British wage for software engineers.[13] The ideology of dispensing with the labour force has spread to the distributive and service industries, to government and local government, and even to those branches of public employment concerned with servicing the needs of impoverished communities. The deprived, and the people charged with serving their needs, find themselves increasingly in the same boat.

It's an absurd and explosive situation, and sooner or later it is going to explode. Just as Michael Young forecast, we are going to see, early in the next century, an alliance of rejected people with dissident intellectuals, mainly women. They will be asserting the aims and values familiar to the whole tradition of anarchist propaganda over the last century which I have deliberately refrained from talking about. There are plenty of histories around. I am concerned with the re-emergence of anarchism in the next century in Britain which is undoubtedly by now the most centralised country in Europe and especially the country where revenue-gathering is most concentrated in the central state. Everyone here will recognise that the level of their local council tax is determined, not by the good or bad management of their local authority, but by central government's manipulation of its budget.

This re-invented anarchism will probably not use that word but will demonstrate some common characteristics with those tendencies known as *basismo* in Latin America, developing as new social movements encompassing "protest and conflict, lobbying and pressuring government agencies and politicians as well as 'self-help' development projects, of which the most frequently cited are popular education, self-built housing, consumer or producer co-operatives and community health care".

I am quoting from David Lehmann's book on *Democracy and Development in Latin America* in which he attempts to classify and describe the multifarious popular movements in that continent, which certainly have resonances for local community activists in this country. He explains that:

> "*Basismo* proclaims its democratic identity, but it distrusts the formal apparatus of the modern state ... emphasising democracy as an educative and solidarity-building activity of face-to-face groups ... Democracy, for a *basista*, is a matter of overcoming, and undermining unwarranted forms of domination. Domination derived from economic power is illegitimate; domination by political power, whatever its origins, is presumed to be self-interested, moved by shadowy levers and motivations. Hence the preference for political activity involving the physical presence of the grassroots, protesting, petitioning and getting in the way of the smooth running of a machine ..."[14]

Lehmann goes to describe how:

> "In the light of these ideological resistances to involvement in formal politics, it is not surprising that communal self-management and 'collective-consumption trade unionism' have become the main practical vehicles of secular *basismo*. Communal self-management is not the same as 'local government' and does not aim to replace local government because it does not have any

pretensions to become an organ of the state; it can rather be described as a proposal of the management of public goods by their beneficiaries. It is a recipe for the proliferation of organisations rather than the accumulation of power: one each in each area for sewage, housing, lighting, education and so on ..."

What does he mean by "collective-consumption trade unionism"? He cites a paper by Robert Wade on 'The management of common property resources: collective action as an alternative to privatisation or state regulation',[15] and explains that:

"'Collective-consumption trade unionism' is not, as its critics sometimes claim, merely another set of pressures place on the hapless representatives of the state to provide anything from schools to transport to urban services and nursery schools. It is also a more sustainable form of unionism because it is built on a tacit assumption of fiscal bankruptcy: in these circumstances to press for and obtain collective goods may improve the quality of life as much as or more than conventional trade-unionist attempts to raise wages – especially in times of inflation. A sewage system is less likely to be eroded by inflation, for example, than a percentage wage increase, though it can hardly be regarded as a substitute for it. Even without inflation, the difficulties of translating private purchasing power into, for example, a sewage system, are substantial: innumerable people with the same purchasing power are also trying to get their hands on the state's depleted budget ... But the pessimistic assumptions of the dilemma do not necessarily hold in a small-scale context where people know each other, and where they have opportunities to learn, and thus to modify their own and each others' behaviour over a period of time."

Most people here will be familiar with one or other of the many studies of popular self-organisation in very poor communities in Latin America, and with Peter Lloyd's description of them as *Slums of Hope*.[16] In the cities of the rich world, the poor are reduced to a condition, not of hope, but of despair. Hence the alienation of the young, positively at war with their environment, and with each other, who are the biggest obstacle to the spread of local self-management and the growth of a community economy among the people who have been cast away by the market and its values.

Kropotkin, whose definition of anarchism I read to you, struggled with this issue and concluded that:

> "Of course in every society, no matter how well organised, people will be found with easily aroused passions, who may, from time to time, commit anti-social deeds. But what is necessary to prevent this is to give their passions a healthy direction, another outlet ... Family life, based on the original community, has disappeared. A new family, based on community of aspirations, will take its place. In this family people will be obliged to know one another, to aid one another and to lean on one another for moral support on every occasion. And this mutual prop will prevent the great number of anti-social acts which we see today."[17]

The wild young men seem to be living out a Wild West scenario of their own, so let me remind you again of the conclusion of that pioneer sociologist Edward Allsworth Ross, and the meaning he gave to the term *social control*, established without the benefit of legal and punitive authority:

> "Sympathy, sociability, the sense of justice and resentment are competent, under favourable circumstances, to work out by themselves a true, natural order, that is to say, an order without design or art."[18]

This is the meaning I ascribe to anarchism in the 21st century. We have to make the circumstances favourable, which they are certainly not today.

Notes and References

1. Peter Kropotkin (1910) article for *Encyclopaedia Britannica*, 11th edition (reprinted in Peter Kropotkin (1984) edited by Nicolas Walter, *Anarchism and Anarchist Communism*, Freedom Press: London).

2. Sam Dogloff (Ed.) (1972) *Bakunin on Anarchy*, Alfred A. Knopf: New York.

3. See Colin Ward (Ed.) Peter Kropotkin (1974) *Fields, Factories and Workshops*, Allen & Unwin: London (Freedom Press, 1984).

4. Michael Young (1958) *The Rise of the Meritocracy*, Penguin Books: Harmondsworth.

5. Will Hutton (1996) 'The 30/30/40 society' in *RSA Journal*, March.

6. Martin Buber (1951) 'Society and the State' in *World Review*, reprinted in Martin Buber (1957) *Pointing the Way*, Routledge & Kegan Paul: London.

7. Robert D. Putnam with Robert Leonardi and Raffaella Y. Nanetti (1993) *Making Democracy Work: Civic Traditions in Modern Italy*, Princeton University Press: New Jersey.

8. Anne Power and Rebecca Tunstall (1995) *Swimming Against the Tide: Polarisation or Progress on 20 Unpopular Council Estates 1980-1995*, Joseph Rowntree Foundation: York.

9. Anne Power (1984) *Area-based Poverty: Social Problems and Resident Empowerment*, (Discussion Paper WSP/107, LSE Welfare State Programme, Room R405A: London).

10. Peter Kellner (1994) 'Don't blame the underclass – the trouble starts at the top', *The Sunday Times*, 29th May.

11. Edward Allsworth Ross, *Social Control*, New York (1901).

12. Stanley Cohen (1985) *Visions of Social Control*, Polity Press: Cambridge.

13. *The Economist*, 23 March 1996.

14. David Lehmann (1990) *Democracy and Development in Latin America*, Polity Press: Cambridge.

15. Robert Wade (1987) 'The management of common property resources: collective action as an alternative to privatisation or state regulation', *Cambridge Journal of Economics*, No. 11.

16. Peter Lloyd (1979) *Slums of Hope? Shanty towns of the third world,* Penguin Books: Harmondsworth.

17. Peter Kropotkin (1877) *Prisons and the Moral Influence on Prisoners,* reprinted in R. Baldwin (Ed.) *Kropotkin's Revolutionary Pamphlets,* Viking: New York (1927) and Dover Books (1968).

18. Ross *op. cit.*

Colin Ward

ANARCHY IN ACTION

In his introduction the author writes: "This book was not intended for people who had spent a lifetime pondering the problems of anarchism, but for those who either had no idea of what the word implied, or who knew exactly what it implied and rejected it, considering that it had no relevance for the modern world.

"My original preference as a title was the more cumbersome but more accurate 'Anarchism as a Theory of Organisation' because, as I urge in my preface, that is what the book is about. It is not about strategies for revolution and it is not involved in speculation on the way an anarchist society would function. It is about the ways in which people organise themselves in any kind of human society, whether we care to categorise those societies as primitive, traditional, capitalist or communist ..."
Anarchy in Action has been published in seven languages.

Some press comments on *Anarchy in Action*

"Readable and refreshing ... his descriptions are always attractive ... his conclusions convincing."
New Society

"Ward has not given us the definitive theory of the alternative society, but he has made a signal contribution to it ... he has brilliantly re-stated anarchism in terms which show its relevance to our present condition."
Peace News

"His arguments become increasingly important as he is able to relate them to present day events..."
The Times Educational Supplement

Revised and re-set fourth impression, 1996

Freedom Press   144 pages   **ISBN 0 900384 20 4**   **£4.95**

Colin Ward

TALKING HOUSES

Some press comments on Colin Ward's *Talking Houses*

"Many will welcome this latest addition to the prolific Ward literature on housing. As the author himself candidly says, these ten lectures merely reiterate the – to him – simple truths he has been proclaiming for the last 45 years. He confesses that he has nothing new to say and it puzzles him that he is in perpetual demand as a pundit. He can only explain it by people wanting hands-on contact with the human propagators of ideas. Always in the vanguard of fresh examples, he does, indeed, continue to have a unique role to play."
Alison Ravetz in *The Architects' Journal*

"Ward believes that when people cooperate on a small scale and choose, manage and even build for themselves, they get better housing than when governments make choices for them. Decades of official directives and central control have kept us from a great state secret: human beings are, unless culturally disabled, well qualified to meet their essential needs – food, shelter and conviviality."
Peter Campbell in *New Statesman and Society*

"The relevance of the anarchist analysis ought to be self-evident ... This book is a valuable source of practical examples of user control and provides glimpses of a well constructed ideological framework to set them in ... conveyed with absolute clarity."
Benjamin Derbyshire in *RIBA Journal*

"Labour's policy on housing has not yet gone on the offensive in reappropriating the language and spirit of self-help and local control so that people no longer fear that regulation is its knee-jerk solution to all problems. The party could usefully borrow from Ward's exhilarating polemic in support of changing the role of the administration from providers to enablers, of the citizens from recipients to participants."
Shaun Spiers in *Tribune*

Freedom Press   **142 pages**   **ISBN 0 900384 55 7**   **£5.00**

Colin Ward

FREEDOM TO GO:
AFTER THE MOTOR AGE

An anarchist approach to the problems of transport. Personal mobility is a priceless human achievement which is a twentieth century disaster: it has destroyed the urban environment, it has cost more lives than modern wars, it has wasted both energy resources and the ozone layer. Can we have the freedom to go and a viable future? This book argues the case for the valid alternatives.

An Italian edition of this book was published in 1992, and reprinted in 1997. A French translation appeared in 1993 and a Spanish version in 1996 .

"Can we outgrow the childhood yearning for the wishmobile – one wish and you are there – the preoccupation with private transport which threatens the well-being of us all? Are there ways for each and all to have the freedom to go without destroying the urban environment, endangering life and wasting energy? The author examines a wide range of possibilities from the libertarian point of view."
Caroline Cahm in *Bus Stop Jottings* (National Federation of Bus Users)

"True to form, Ward has produced a thought-provoking mixture of idealism and common sense. The source of his enduring optimism, that the human spirit will triumph over the dehumanising forces at large in the world, is a mystery; but in this book, as in his journalism, I find it inspiring."
Professor John Adams in *The Architects' Journal*

Freedom Press   112 pages   ISBN 0 900384 61 1   £3.50